Carving Carousel Animals

From ⅛ Scale to Full Size

Carving Carousel Animals

From ⅛ Scale to Full Size

H. LeRoy Marlow

Sterling Publishing Co., Inc.   New York

ACKNOWLEDGMENTS

Appreciation is expressed to Mrs. Martie Mensch,
for the professional manner in which she handled the
word processing duties, and Mr. David G. Shelly,
for the excellent photographs.

Edited by Michael Cea

Library of Congress Cataloging-in-Publication Data
Marlow, H. LeRoy.
    Carving carousel animals : from 1/8 scale to full size / H. LeRoy
Marlow.
        p.   cm.
    Includes index.
    ISBN 0-8069-6802-8
    1. Wood-carving.   2. Merry-go-round art.   3. Animals in art.
I. Title.   II. Title: Carousel animals.
TT199.7.M37   1989   88-37050
731′.8323—dc19   CIP

Table of Contents

DEDICATION

For my wife, Mildred, with love,
for her patience in picking up
countless chips of wood.

Illus. 1. Author H. LeRoy Marlow posing with a full-size lead horse.
Instructions for making full-size carousel animals are given on pages
162–189.

Introduction

Our nation is currently experiencing a renewed interest in the carousel. Many of us cherish memories of hours of riding pleasure on the carousel when we were young. This amusement ride, which reached its greatest popularity during the first quarter of this century, is now being displayed in museums and art galleries. The hand-carved animals which were thought of as merely components on the carousel have become works of art and collector's items.

The carousel or its forerunner has been around since the Byzantine period. The animals have evolved from relatively simple forms to elaborately carved and bejewelled figures. The carvers at first created the animals in their spare time, but as the popularity of the carousel increased skilled carvers from the wagon, ship-building, furniture, architectural, and other industries devoted their talents to creating carousel horses and goats, camels, lions, tigers, frogs, cats, dogs, and other animals referred to as menagerie animals. The names of the individual carvers are largely unknown today because they very seldom signed their work, yet the names of the companies which produced the carousels have been preserved.

Unlike other products that were manufactured, no blue prints were made of the carousel animals. Only large patterns or sketches, often made on brown wrapping paper or cardboard, guided the carver. Working as a team headed by a master carver, the crew would rough-carve the animals and the master carver would decide on the final details. To aid production, standardized leg and body positions were often used. As the industry grew, much of the initial hand work was eliminated as the rough carvings were produced mechanically.

Reproductions of animals produced by the Herschell-Spillman Company of Towanda, New York were selected for this book because I grew up riding on their carvings and fell in love with them. Even today I favor the work of this company over some other companies. However, since people have an emotional attachment to carousel animals, just about everyone has a favorite style. You may be partial to the work of Dentzel, Looff, Illions, Parker, Muller, Zalar, or someone else; if so, the procedures outlined in this book to duplicate their work will apply just as well. You can even use these procedures to create your own original animals.

Since no shop drawings were available, templates for each of the major parts were made. Many of the templates were destroyed by fire or were discarded when a carousel manufacturing company ceased operation. To aid you in carving, one-eighth scale line drawings have been provided for the 31 animals selected. These plans constitute the only known set of detailed scale drawings of carousel figures available today.

The projects in this book are intended as a challenge for those individuals with some skill and experience as wood-carvers. Each line drawing has a series of grid points which will help you to reproduce a figure from the one-eighth-scale shown on each plan to a full-size animal or any size in between. This flexibility of scale is important since many carousel lovers have limited space where they can display the finished carving. While theoretically it is possible to make a carving smaller than one-eighth scale, and the outlined procedures will help you do it, it is not recommended because much of the detail will be lost.

There is a black-and-white photo accompanying the instructions for most of the carousel animals. These projects will also be represented in the color section. Unfortunately, a few of these projects do not have any photographs. In these cases, you will be able to determine the detail of the carousel animal through the line drawings presented.

The carvings in this book are not designed to be weekend projects. The carving time for a scale-size animal may range from 12 to 45 hours, and that for a full-size animal as much as ten times longer. For those willing to make the commitment, the results are well worth the effort.

Happy carving.

H. LeRoy Marlow

SCALE-SIZE CAROUSEL ANIMALS

Carving Techniques

his chapter presents procedures, techniques, ideas, and tips that will prove helpful when you carve any carousel animal you select. The information applies equally well to the animals presented in the following pages and to your own creations.

DEVELOPING THE PLAN

If you should elect to carve one of the animals presented on pages 22–160, then the plan is already developed and you only have to follow the construction details presented in this chapter.

If you want to develop your own plan for a favorite carousel animal, you have two choices. If you are a talented artist, you can make an original sketch of the animal to the desired size. However, if you are not that artistically inclined, you can still develop or customize a plan. Visit a carousel and select the animal that you want to carve. Take a 2 × 2 color slide of the romance side. The romance side, for American carousels, will be the right side of the animal. This side is elaborately carved, has the most trappings and, for the animals on the outside row, will usually display jewels. American carousels rotate counterclockwise, so the romance side is the one that potential riders see before they board the ride.

To get the most practical photograph, make sure that the camera angle is perpendicular to the side of the animal and at a level that's approximately at the midpoint of the animal. To assist you later when you are carving, it is wise to also take a series of photographs showing the front, rear, inside, and details of the selected animal.

Measure the distance between two critical points, such as the distance from the bottom of the shoe to the top of the ear, bottom of the shoe to top of the saddle, or rump to breast. Convert this measurement to the appropriate scale dimension. For example, the actual measurement of the lead horse (Illus. 9) from the bottom of the shoe to the top of the ear is 56″. For a one-eighth-scale model, this dimension will be 7″.

On a piece of 8½ × 11″ plain white paper draw two horizontal parallel lines 7″ apart. Project the slide image of the animal that you have photographed (in this case, the lead horse) onto the piece of paper. Adjust the focal length and focus so that the tip of the ear touches one horizontal line and the bottom of the shoe touches the other. Trace the outline and details of the projected animal.

Examine the drawing of the body, head, tail, and legs and decide the best direction the wood grain should go. Mark the places where joints should be made (see Illus. 9 as an example). You now have a working plan.

PREPARING THE CARVING BLOCK

Using one of the plans provided on pages 22–160 or one that you have developed, cut out the patterns for the parts—the head, body, legs, and tail. Using rubber cement, adhere the patterns onto wood of the correct thickness and size as given for each animal. In order for your finished carving to maintain all the fine details without splitting, select a close-grain wood like basswood. Pay particular attention to the direction of the grain. To provide maximum strength, the grain should run lengthwise on the part as noted in each parts list.

Using a coping saw or jigsaw, cut out the outline of each part. Drill a ³⁄₁₆″ hole through the body; you will use this hole later to insert a dowel that will constitute the pole.

With the patterns still glued to the wood, glue the parts together to complete the total carving block. Because you will be gluing end grain, which absorbs glue rapidly, it is important that you "size" or "butter" the parts prior to final gluing. To do this, place a thin film of glue on the end grain. Wipe off the excess glue and let the glue dry. Apply glue to the surfaces to be joined, press the parts together, and let the glue set.

The type of glue used may be left to the preference of the carver. However, ready-to-use glues offer the greatest convenience. White all-purpose glue is probably the most popular, and it will do a very satisfactory job of adhering wood. However, yellow carpenter's glue was developed especially for wood, and is, therefore, recommended. This glue "grabs" faster than white glue, a characteristic helpful in preparing carving blocks. The drying time is approximately 45–60 minutes at 70° F. Increasing the temperature will reduce the time required for the glue to set.

One note of caution, however, should be heeded for yellow glue. The pieces to be joined, the glue, and the work area must be at least 65° F or a good bond may not result.

Although it is possible to carve each animal from a solid block, much of the cutting would have to be done across the grain; this is not recommended for these delicate carvings. The finished animal would possess many structural weaknesses. Time and effort can be saved, and a stronger carving produced, if the parts are "glued up."

However, this procedure is used when the finished carving will be painted. If the carving is to be left natural, then you can carve it from a solid block of wood despite the inherent grain weaknesses.

Illus. 2. One-eighth-scale pig with its legs glued in place and ready for carving. Note the direction of the grain.

CARVING THE ANIMAL

An experienced wood-carver will have his or her own method of carving. I have found it helpful to leave the patterns glued to the sides of the animal and stop-cut the major components. Then I proceed to round the animal by roughly cutting it to shape. This step is referred to as "boasting," and is a preliminary step to the finer work that will follow.

The dimensions shown in each table of critical dimensions provide reference points to aid in carving. It is not possible to mark each detail, but if you use the line drawings, photographs, and critical dimensions as references, the proper relationships between the component parts can be maintained.

In most cases, the initial glued-up block will be complete and it will only be necessary to carve away and "release" the animal that is being held within. In some cases, you may want to carve a part separately and then add it on. Such is the case for the rings on the side of the camel (Illus. 39). In every case where parts are added to the initial block, a notation has been added to the instructions. After all the carving is completed, sand the animal to prepare it for painting.

THE FINISHING TOUCHES

When the carving is complete, there are several other things that can be done to provide additional realism. They are discussed below.

Building a Stand

A base to keep the carved carousel figure upright will be needed. This base can be a simple block, an elaborate turning, or some other stand that you will enjoy. However, the completed carousel animal will look more realistic if it is mounted on an appropriate base. The

Illus. 3. One-eighth-scale lead horse partially carved and ready for the finishing details.

base suggested in Illus. 4 is in scale with the one-eighth size line drawings in this book. It represents a scale segment of the full-size carousel platform.

The length of each base is determined by the length of each animal as suggested in Table 1. Using Illus. 4 as a reference, start at the extreme left point of the longitudinal centerline and draw a line equal to the length of chord A for the selected animal. (For some of the longer animals it will be necessary to glue together two copies of Illus. 4.) Draw a radial line through the point just established and intersect the front and back edges. This determines the length of the stand.

The location of the 3⁄16″ hole for the pole is determined in a similar manner. (The position for the hole is on the longitudinal centerline and located so that there will be approximately 1⁄2″ in front and behind the figure. This is arbitrary and you can change the dimensions to suit your taste.) Again starting at the extreme left of the longitudinal centerline, measure the distance of chord B. This will determine the location of the pole hole.

Cut the crescent-shaped base from 1⁄2″ stock. Glue flooring fashioned from stock 1⁄16″ thick × 1⁄4″ wide × random lengths on top of the base. Most of the floorboards run parallel to each other, but there should be a curved finishing piece on the front and back. The front curved finishing piece should overhang the base by 1⁄16″. It will be necessary to shape the floorboards where they meet the finishing pieces. The edges of each piece of flooring should be bevelled slightly so that the floorboard effect will be obvious in the finished base.

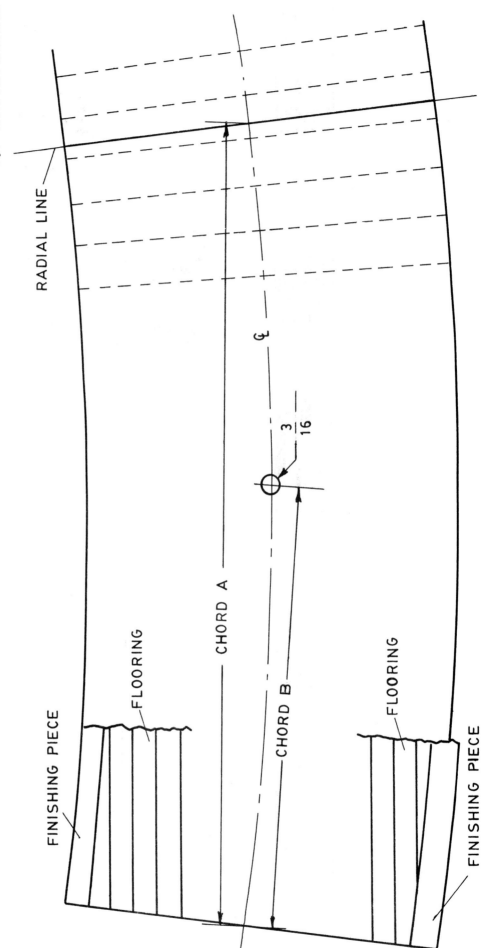

Illus. 4. Stand for scale-size animals.

RADIAL LINE

FINISHING PIECE

FLOORING

CHORD A

$\frac{3}{16}$

₵

CHORD B

FLOORING

FINISHING PIECE

Table 1   Suggested Dimensions for Scale Animal Stands

Animal	Length Chord A	Pole Hole Chord B
Lead Horse	8³⁄₁₆″	4⁹⁄₁₆″
Sea Monster	9⁷⁄₈″	5¹⁄₁₆″
Parrot Horse	9¾″	5⅜″
Goat	8¾″	4¾″
King's Horse	9¼″	5⅛″
Stork	7½″	4⅝″
Sheik's Horse	9″	5⁵⁄₁₆″
Lion	12¹⁄₁₆″	7¼″
Gladiator Horse	8½″	4¹⁵⁄₁₆″
Standing White Horse	9⅜″	5⁷⁄₁₆″
Tiger	9⁷⁄₈″	5¹⁵⁄₁₆″
Horse with Green Blanket	9¾″	5⁷⁄₁₆″
Camel	9¼″	5⅛″
Brown Horse	7¾″	4½″
Reindeer	8¾″	5⅜″
Horse with Feathers	8½″	4⅞″
Giraffe	8⅞″	4⅝″
Ostrich	6⁹⁄₁₆″	3⅞″
Jumper with Red Blanket	7¼″	3¹⁵⁄₁₆″
Mule	8¹³⁄₁₆″	4¾″
Horse with Plaid Blanket	7⅜″	4¼″
Horse with Orange Streamers	7½″	4″
Rooster	8⅛″	5″
Indian Horse	8⅜″	4¹³⁄₁₆″
American Jumper	8″	4¾″
Pig	7⅜″	4⁵⁄₁₆″
Black Beauty	6⅞″	4³⁄₁₆″
Zebra	6⅞″	4⁵⁄₁₆″
Cat	8⅞″	5⁵⁄₁₆″
Frog	6⅜″	3⅝″
Dog	8⅝″	4⅞″

Placing each piece of flooring separately involves extra time and effort, but the final result is well worth it. If you want to take a shortcut, you can achieve a similar effect by merely scoring the finishing pieces and floorboards onto the ½″ thick base. In this case, there will not be an overhang and the final effect will not be as pleasing, but it will take less time.

A mahogany stain and satin varnish provide a nice finish for the base. When the edge of the overhang is painted a brilliant color, it highlights the carving.

Some carousels have a plain painted floor, and you may elect to forego the floorboards and merely paint the base; in this case, select a color that will complement and not distract from the carving.

Pole And Footrest

The pole for each one-eighth scale carousel animal is a 10¼″ length of ³⁄₁₆″ dowel. The pole should be painted gold. On some animals, a scale footrest can be added. Two footrests are shown in Illus. 5. One has been enlarged for the sake of clarity; the other, full-sized, can be used as a pattern.

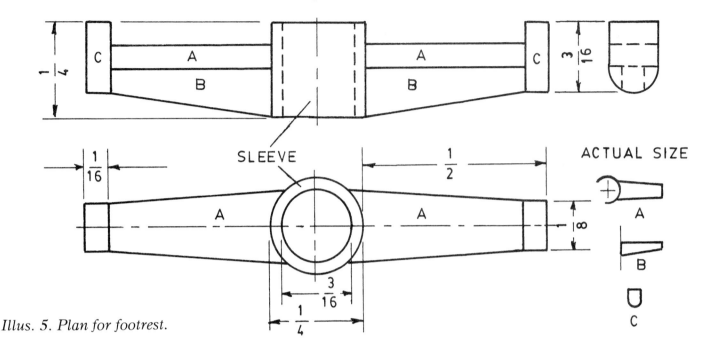

Illus. 5. Plan for footrest.

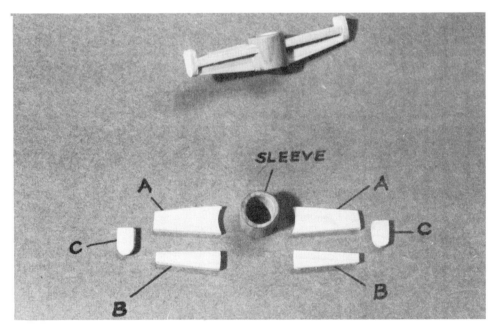

Illus. 6. Footrest showing the component parts and the complete assembly.

The sleeve is the central part for each footrest. It is a hollowed-out ¼″ segment of a ¼″ dowel to which the other footrest parts are glued. It has close tolerances, and can be made successfully by the following procedure: Clamp a piece of ¾″ scrap stock on the drill press table. Drill a ¼″ perpendicular hole into the scrap. Do not move the scrap wood or change the drill press setting. Replace the ¼″ drill with a ³⁄₁₆″ drill. Place a short length of a ¼″ dowel—about 1″—into the hole in the scrap wood. Drill a ³⁄₁₆″ hole into the dowel.

Since the setup has not changed, the ³⁄₁₆″ hole will be centered in the ¼″ dowel. If you feel that you need a little more room for error, or if the pole dowel is oversized, substitute a ⁵⁄₁₆″ dowel for the sleeve.

Use a very fine blade (30 teeth to the inch, .018″ thick, and .042″ wide) in the jigsaw and cut the hollow dowel into ¼″ lengths. To minimize breakage, insert a ³⁄₁₆″ dowel in the hole while cutting the sleeve to length.

Using Illus. 5 as a pattern, cut out of ¹⁄₁₆″ stock two each of parts A, B, and C. Glue part B perpendicular to A. Glue part C to the narrow end of A and B, as shown. Wrap sandpaper around the ¼″ dowel and shape the wide end of A-B to conform to the sleeve. Glue the assembled parts (A, B, and C) to each side of the sleeve. Slide the completed footstep onto the pole and glue it approximately ¹³⁄₁₆″ below the belly of the animal.

Painting

A few collectors of carousel animals like to have the carvings unfinished, but most collectors respond very positively to the traditional bright colors. With very few exceptions, it is impossible to positively determine the original colors of the animals. The animals were usually given a fresh coat of paint, mostly applied by unskilled workmen, at the start of each carnival or fair season. It is not unusual to find old carousel animals with as many as 30 coats of paint, which have often obliterated the fine details of the original carving.

The decision as to what type of paint you should use is entirely up to you. However, I have had good success with regular household enamels. The animals shown in the color section were finished with gloss paints that are available from any hardware dealer. These paints are ideal to use on the carousel animal for the following reasons: (1) they come in brilliant colors; (2) they can be easily mixed to the desired shade; (3) they do not dry too rapidly; (4) they provide a very durable finish; (5) they are safe; and (6) you do not have to be an accomplished artist to get very pleasing results.

Many of the carousel animals that are being restored today are being painted by artists who are adding their own creative touches, which include pastel colors, the blending of many colors, and shading. You can use these touches in the color scheme of your completed carving if you desire. I lean towards minimizing the air-brushing of the carvings and painting them with clearly defined color separations, as shown in the color section.

I have found it helpful to start the painting process by applying a base coat to the entire carving. The color of this coat should usually be the body color of the animal. By painting the entire animal, you cover many of the minute cracks and depressions, which will make it easier for you when you paint the details later.

A suggested color scheme for painting is offered for each animal. The symbols on all of the plans are as follow:

(B)—Black (gloss)
(BF)—Black (flat)
(BK)—Blue (dark)
(BL)—Blue (light)
(BN)—Brown (dark)
(BR)—Brown (light)
(C)—Cream
(F)—Flesh
(G)—Gold
(GE)—Green (dark)
(GF)—Green (light)
(GR)—Grey

(GS)—Green Stain
(MS)—Mahogany Stain
(O)—Orange
(OL)—Olive
(OW)—Off White
(P)—Pink
(R)—Red
(RU)—Rust
(S)—Silver
(T)—Tan
(W)—White
(Y)—Yellow

The final color selection should be yours, and the animal painted in colors that you find pleasing, harmonious, and satisfying.

Jewels

The animals on the inside rows do not have jewels. All of the animals on the outside row (except the sea monster and the stork) have jewels on at least one place on the romance side, and many have them on the saddle, head, neck, and rear flank.

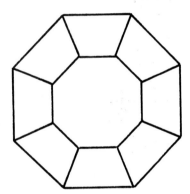

Rhinestones are excellent to use as jewels on the one-eighth-scale carvings because you can usually get them in the desired colors and because their diameters are in scale with the diameters of the original jewels. Suppliers of 1-mm–4-mm rhinestones are listed in the Suppliers List on page 191. (These rhinestones are sold in millimetres, and when I refer to them in text, I will use their metric sizes.) These companies may carry either the flat-back or pointed-back rhinestones. Flat stones, which are glued to the surface of the carving, are not as attractive on the finished carving as the pointed ones, which can be set into the carvings.

Rhinestones with pointed backs are shown in Illus. 7. When using this type of rhinestone, you can make a cone-shaped hole of the proper size in the final carving by using a high-speed cone-shaped steel cutter in a hand-held motor tool. If you cannot locate rhinestones with pointed backs, use flat-back stones.

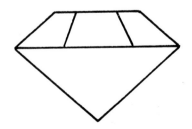

Illus. 7. Rhinestone with pointed back.

I have successfully located pointed rhinestones in old costume jewelry at flea markets. The newer costume jewelry does not work as well since the jewels are fused into the setting; however, older jewelry was made differently and you can pop out the stone without damaging it.

A suggested color scheme for rhinestones is offered for each animal. The symbols shown on the plans are as follow:

A—Amber	BK—Blue (Dark)	G—Green	V—Violet
B—Blue	C—Clear Crystal	R—Red	

The Outside Row

American carousels rotate counterclockwise, so the right side of each animal—the romance side—is the one which is elaborately carved and decorated. This is the side that will be displayed most often in the finished carving; however, to complete the carving it will be necessary for you to also see the other side. Therefore, the plans for each animal show the inside as well as the romance side.

The instructions provided on pages 12–20 apply to each carving and will not be repeated here. In every case you will have to do the following: (1) use the plan and cut out the pattern for each part; (2) adhere the patterns to wood of the proper thickness with the correct grain orientation; (3) jigsaw to shape the outer edges; (4) drill the 3/16" hole for the pole; (5) glue up the carving block; (6) do the initial stop-carving, round the animal, and complete the details; (7) finish-sand the carving; and (8) paint in selected colors.

This section presents the plans, dimensions and photographs needed to carve a one-eighth-scale replica of the larger and more elaborate animals located on the outside row of the carousel.

Lead Horse

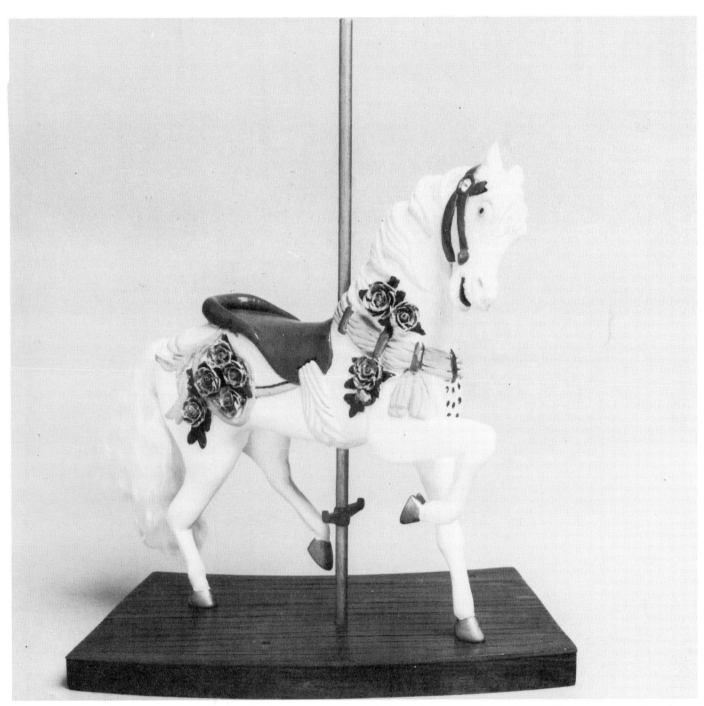

Illus. 8. On every carousel there is one animal—usually a horse—that is more elaborately decorated and is the highlight of the ride. Such a carving is designated as the lead horse. For a look at the lead horse in full color, turn to page I of the Color Section.

DIRECTIONS

Using Illus. 9 as a plan, cut out the ten patterns and glue each pattern to wood of the correct thickness as defined in Table 2. You will have to refer to Illus. 10 for the complete pattern for the left legs. The length of each part should follow the direction of the grain.

Table 2 Parts List for the Lead Horse

Part	*Length*	*Width*	*Thickness*
Head	2⅜″	1⅛″	⅞″
Body	6⁵⁄₁₆″	4¹⁄₁₆″	1⅜″
Right Front Leg	1½″	⁷⁄₁₆″	⅜″
Right Front Hoof	⅞″	⅜″	⅜″
Left Front Leg	3⅛″	1″	½″
Right Hind Thigh	1⅝″	1½″	⅝″
Right Hind Leg/Hoof	1⅝″	⁷⁄₁₆″	⅜″
Left Hind Thigh	2″	1⅛″	⅝″
Left Hind Leg	1¼″	⅜″	⅜″
Left Hind Hoof	¹¹⁄₁₆″	⅜″	⅜″

The complete carving block consists of ten parts, as follow: head, body, right front leg (2 sections), left front leg, right hind leg (2 sections), and left hind leg (3 sections). Drill a ³⁄₁₆″ hole through the body for the pole and the ⅛″ hole for the tail before gluing the head and legs in place. Size the end grain of each part and glue the head and legs to the body. The head tilts sideways 33° to the right.

Make the nine roses from ¹⁄₃₂″ stock (veneer) and glue them in place. Cut out four horseshoes from ¹⁄₁₆″ stock and glue one to the bottom of each foot. Refer to Illus. 8–10 and Table 3 to complete the final shapes and details. The approximate carving time is 45 hours.

The following table provides the critical dimensions that you will need when carving a ⅛-scale or full-size model:

Table 3 Critical Dimensions for the Lead Horse

	⅛ Scale	*Full Size*
Bottom of shoe to top of ear	7″	56″
Width of head	⅞″	7″
Width of mouth	⁵⁄₁₆″	2½″
Width of nose	⁷⁄₁₆″	3½″
Distance between eyes	¾″	6″
Distance between tips of ears	¹⁹⁄₃₂″	4¾″
Width of neck at ribbon	1⅛″	9″
Width of body at pole	1⅜″	11″
Width of rear flank	1⁵⁄₁₆″	10½″
Width of saddle at rear	1⅜″	11″
Width of front leg at body	½″	4″
Width of hind leg at body	⅝″	5″
Width of leg at knee	⅜″	3″
Width of hoof	⅜″	3″
Length of hoof	¹⁵⁄₃₂″	3¾″
Distance between front hooves	¾″	6″
Distance between hind hooves	⅝″	5″

After carving, paint in accordance with the suggested color symbols or according to your own taste. Glue a 4-mm crystal rhinestone to

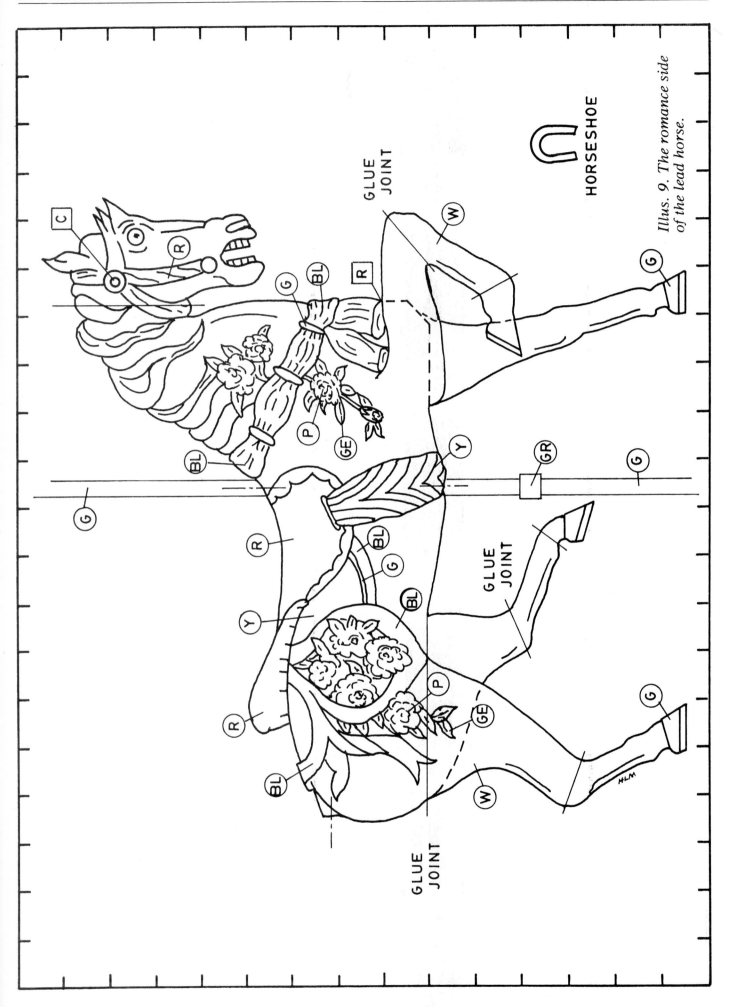

HORSESHOE

GLUE JOINT

GLUE JOINT

GLUE JOINT

Illus. 9. The romance side of the lead horse.

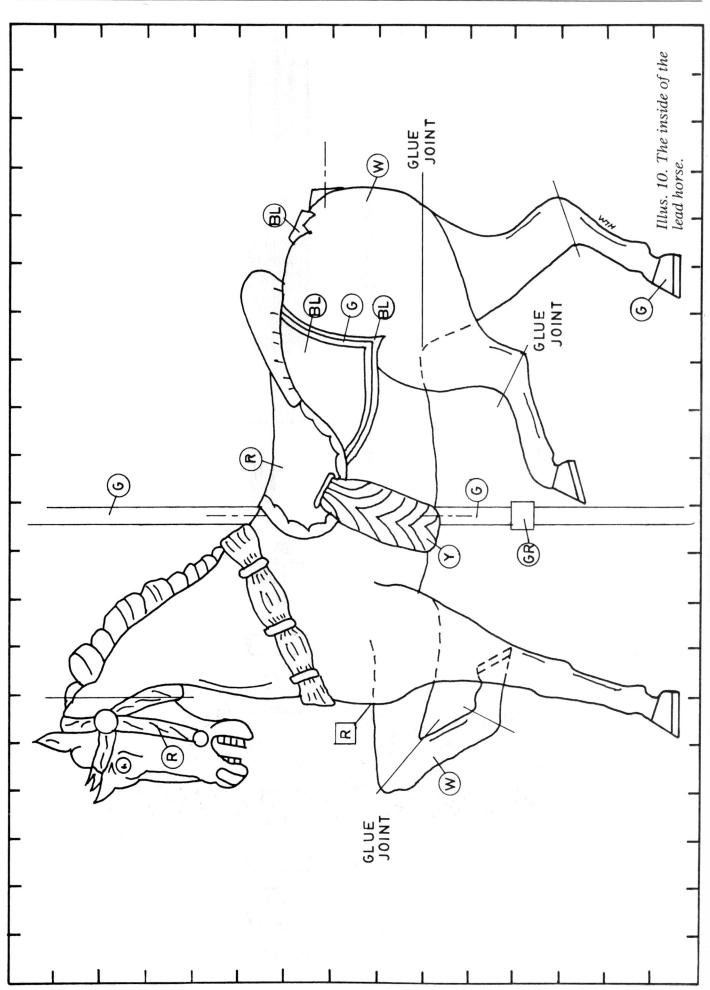

Illus. 10. The inside of the lead horse.

the headband and eleven 2-mm red rhinestones and one 3-mm red rhinestone to the breast ribbon. Make the tail from 2½″ length of white ³⁄₁₆″ nylon rope which you have unravelled, and glue it into the ⅛″ hole in the body. (There are no standard lengths or fullnesses for the tails on carousel animals. The instructions I give you here and in the following projects are for tails of lengths and fullnesses that I have found appealing. You yourself should determine if you want to taper the tail or make it longer, shorter, thinner, or thicker than I have instructed.)

Insert a 10¼″ length of ³⁄₁₆″ dowel through the hole in the body so that 5¼″ extend above the saddle. Glue it in place and add the footrest (Illus. 5) to the pole. Make a stand and glue the pole of the completed horse to it.

Sea Monster

Illus. 11. This animal is mythical and a figment of the imagination of the master carver who created it. It rests on its tail and is supported by the pole. For a look at the sea monster in full color, turn to page G of the Color Section.

DIRECTIONS

Using Illus. 12 as a plan, cut out the outline of the entire animal. Attach the bottom of the tail at line A–B and glue this two-part pattern to a block of wood 8¹¹⁄₁₆″ long × 7⅞″ wide × 1¾″ thick. Make sure that the grain runs horizontally. The head should face straight ahead without any sideways tilt. Drill a ³⁄₁₆″ hole for the pole.

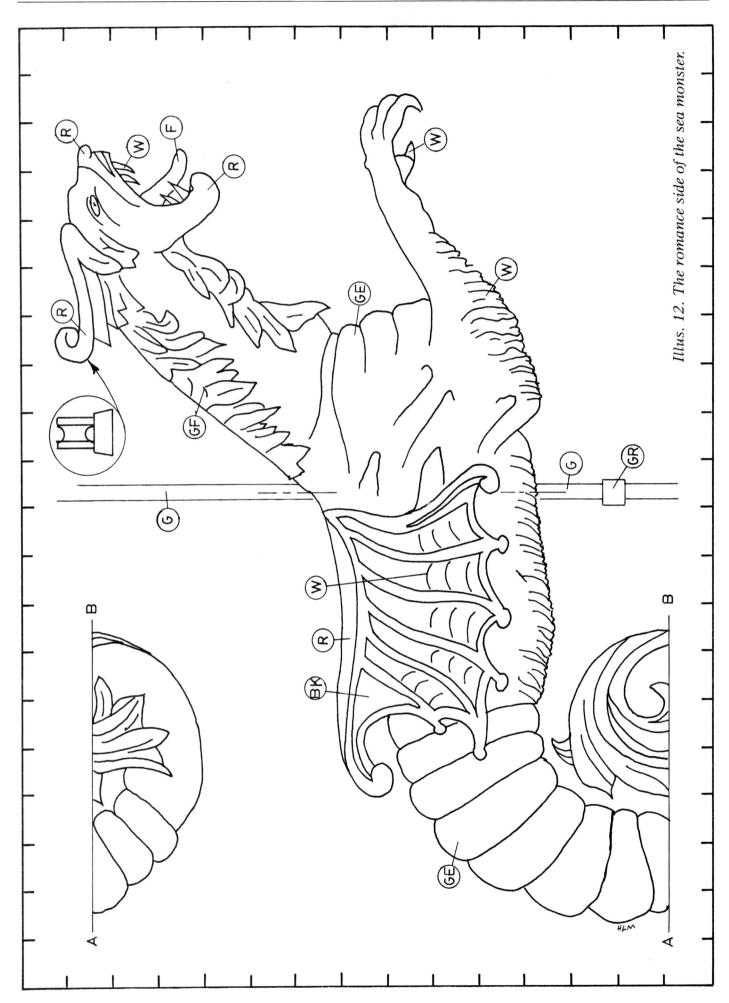

Illus. 12. The romance side of the sea monster.

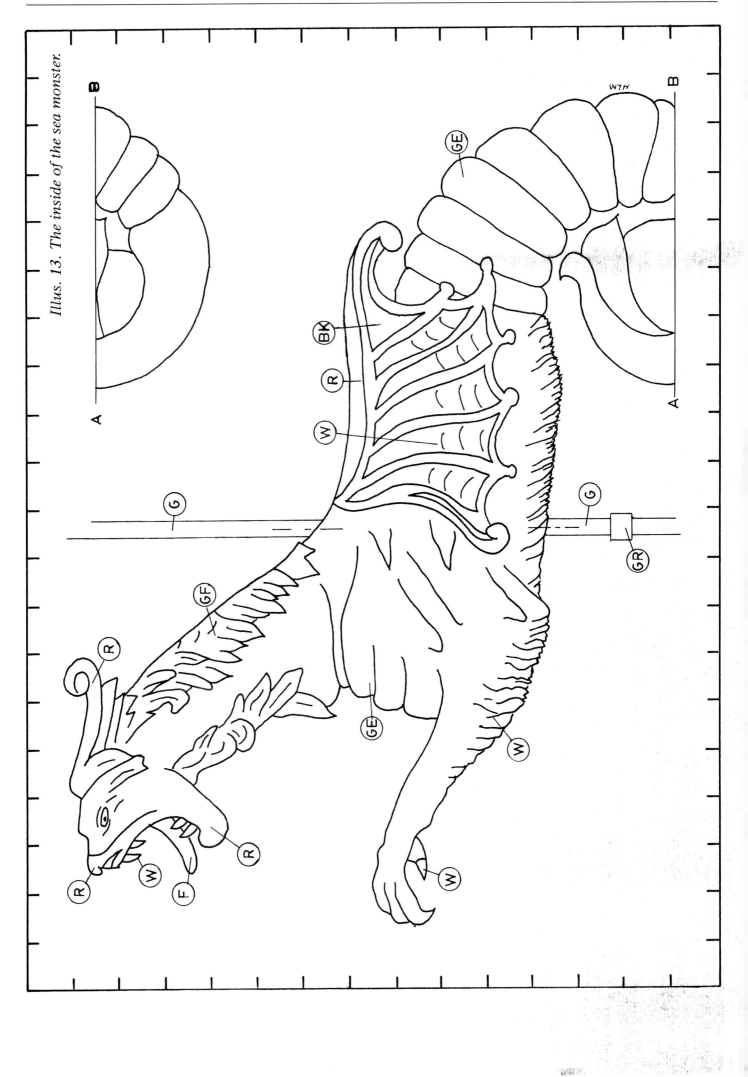

Illus. 13. The inside of the sea monster.

The curl at the bottom of the tail is reduced in thickness to ⅜″ at its top and tilts towards the romance side. The top of the crown has a curved channel in the center of its width, as shown in Illus. 12. Refer to Illus. 11–13 and Table 4 to complete the final shapes and details. The carving time is approximately 29 hours.

The following table provides the critical dimensions that you will need when carving a ⅛-scale or full-size model:

Table 4   Critical Dimensions for the Sea Monster

	⅛ Scale	Full Size
Bottom of tail to top of crown	7⅞″	63″
Width of body at pole	1½″	12″
Width at shoulders	1¾″	14″
Width of neck at body	1⅛″	9″
Width of saddle at rear	1¼″	10″
Width of head	1⅜″	11″
Width of jaw	½″	4″
Width of nose	¾″	6″
Width of tongue	½″	4″
Distance between eyes	1¼″	10″
Width of claws	¾″	6″
Distance between claws	⅝″	5″
Width of tail (front)	½″	4″
Width of tail (rear of saddle)	1¼″	10″
Width of tail (rear at floor)	¾″	6″

After carving, paint in accordance with suggested color symbols or in colors that appeal to you. One interesting treatment is to use green stain for the body and cover it with gloss varnish. This finish gives the animal a wet look.

There are no rhinestones on the sea monster. Insert a 10¼″ length of ³⁄₁₆″ dowel through the hole in the body so that it extends ½″ below the tail. Glue it in place and add the footrest (Illus. 5). Make a stand and place the pole of the completed carving in the base.

Parrot Horse

GENERAL NOTES

This elaborately carved horse, shown in Illus. 14 and 15, is distinguished by the parrot, which actually forms part of the saddle. It gives the rider the illusion of racing ahead at a very rapid speed, rather than the up-and-down motion that is typical of most flying horses.

DIRECTIONS

Using Illus. 14 as a plan, cut out the ten patterns and glue each pattern to wood of the correct thickness as defined in Table 5. The length of each part should follow the direction of the grain.

Table 5   Parts List for the Parrot Horse

Part	Length	Width	Thickness
Head	3⅝″	1⅜″	1″
Body	6¹³⁄₁₆″	2⅝″	1⁷⁄₁₆″
Right Front Leg	1½″	⁷⁄₁₆″	½″
Right Front Hoof	¾″	½″	½″
Left Front Leg	3″	¾″	½″
Right Hind Thigh	1⅛″	⅞″	¾″
Right Hind Leg	2¼″	⁹⁄₁₆″	½″
Left Hind Thigh	1⅜″	1″	¾″
Left Hind Leg	1⅝″	½″	½″
Left Hind Hoof	⅞″	½″	½″

The complete carving block consists of ten parts, as follow: head, body, right front leg (2 sections), left front leg, right hind leg (2 sections), and left hind leg (3 sections). Drill a ³⁄₁₆″ hole through the body for the pole and the ⅛″ hole for the tail before gluing the head and legs to the body. Size the body end grain of each leg part and glue the head and legs in place. The head should be turned 5° to the right.

Cut out four horseshoes from ¹⁄₁₆″ stock and glue one to the bottom of each foot. Refer to Illus. 14, 15, and Table 6 to complete the final shapes and details. The approximate carving time is 40 hours.

Table 6, on page 34, provides the critical dimensions that you will need when carving a ⅛-scale or full-size model.

After carving, paint in accordance with the suggested color symbols or according to your taste. Glue one 3-mm blue rhinestone to the headband, nine 2-mm blue rhinestones to the neckband, eight 2-mm crystal rhinestones to the breast collar, seventeen 2-mm amber rhinestones to the rear right side, and six 2-mm amber rhinestones to the top of the rear flank. Make the tail from approximately 60 pieces of heavy-duty black sewing thread; each piece should be 3″ long.

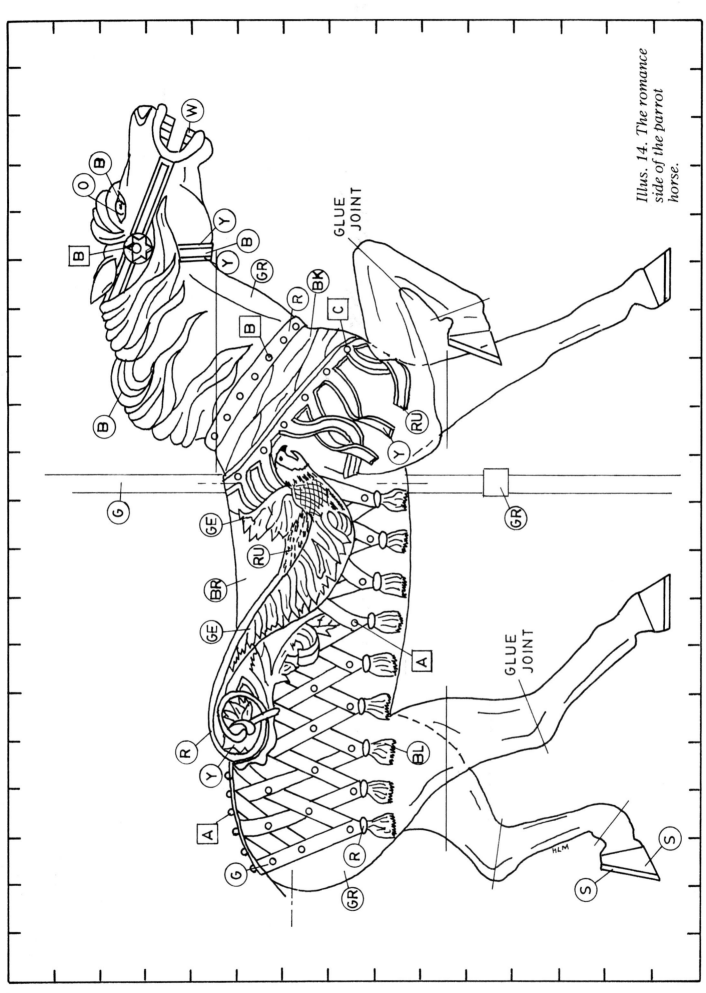

Illus. 14. The romance side of the parrot horse.

GLUE JOINT

GLUE JOINT

Author H. LeRoy Marlow posing with a full-size lead horse.

The close-ups on this and the following page show rose details on the full-size lead horse.

This crafty pig, one of the animals on the inner row of the carousel, is escaping with an ear of corn.

This colorful rooster appears to be trying to take flight.

This dapper frog—clad in jackets and pants—was inspired by Wind in the Willows.

This black-and-white dog is one of several domestic animals that appear on the carousel. Note the series of "diamonds" around the collar on its neck.

The tiger is perhaps the most intricately detailed of the animals. Note the unusual carving of a mermaid on its side.

This cat—outfitted with a bow around its neck—appears to be springing gracefully into the air.

This sea monster is an imaginative and awesome-looking creation. The top of its crown has a curved channel in the center of its width. The curl at the bottom of the tail tilts towards the romance side (the right side on American carousels).

H

No carousel is complete without a patriotic theme. This leaping horse proudly carries the American flag.

The gold mane on this white horse stands out in wonderful contrast.

The lead horse is the most elaborately decorated animal on the carousel.

The mule, another domestic animal, appears on the inner row of the carousel. Its head has a sideways tilt of 5° to the right.

The stork is a classical favorite. Note the unusual position of the baby: on the stork's side, rather than in its beak.

Young children flock to this colorful ostrich. The feathers are shaped with a veining tool, and the veining lines are made with a woodburning pen.

The giraffe is easily the tallest animal on the carousel. Because of its two-tone skin, it takes almost as much time to paint as it does to carve.

The lion is the largest and the most majestic of the felines represented on the carousel.

This zebra was obviously hard to tame, because it has no saddle. It is the least elaborate animal on the carousel.

This Indian's horse is a slice out of the American past. The rope and feathers on the arrows are carved with a knife, and the final details added with a wood-burning pen.

The camel, the most reliable means of transportation in the desert, makes a fun-to-ride carousel animal.

This horse, covered in armor, is ready to carry the king into battle. The individual leaves of the armor can be carved with a veiner gouge.

With its prance-like gait, this goat appears anxious to carry its rider away. The fleece on its body can be simulated by using a cone-shaped steel cutter in a hand-held motor tool.

This reindeer, with a magnificent rack of antlers, is another children's favorite.

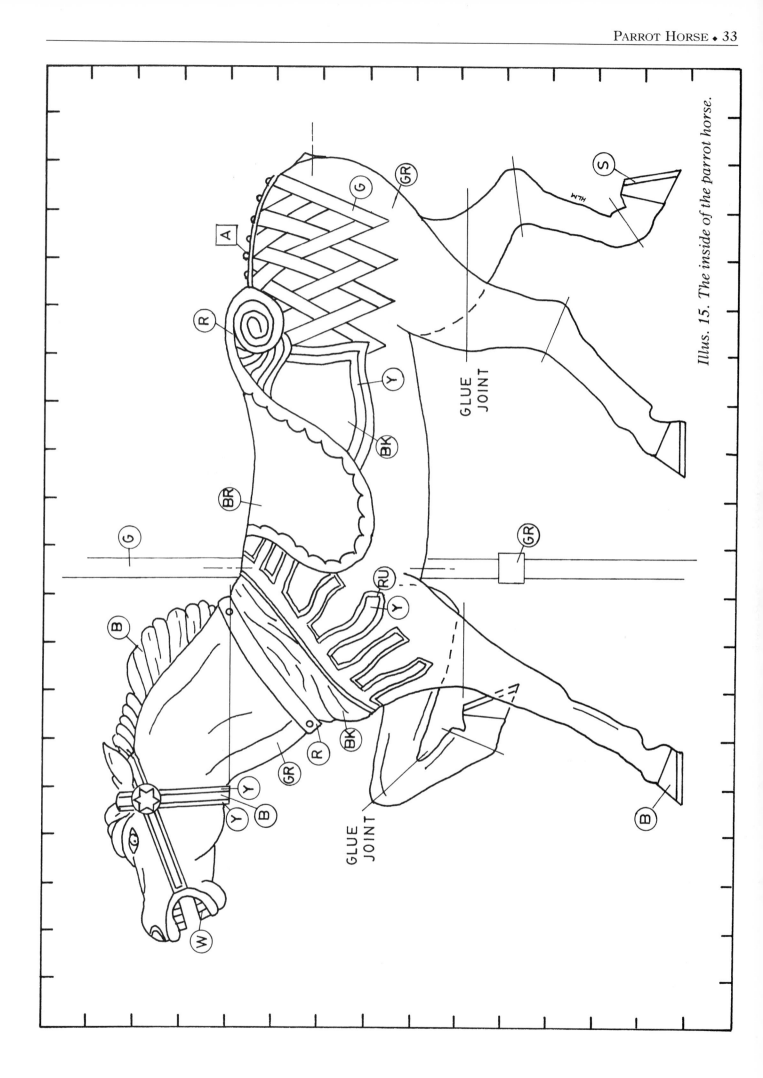

Illus. 15. The inside of the parrot horse.

Insert a 10¼″ length of ³⁄₁₆″ dowel through the hole in the body so that 4⅞″ extend above the saddle. Glue it in place and add the footrest (Illus. 5) to the pole. Make a stand and glue the pole of the completed horse to it.

Table 6   Critical Dimensions for the Parrot Horse

	⅛ Scale	Full Size
Bottom of shoe to top of ear	6⅜″	51″
Width of head (including mane)	1″	8″
Width of head (without mane)	¾″	6″
Width of nose	½″	4″
Distance between eyes	¾″	6″
Distance between tips of ears	¾″	6″
Width of neck at breast collar	¹⁵⁄₁₆″	7½″
Width of body at pole	1⁷⁄₁₆″	11½″
Width of rear flank	1⁷⁄₁₆″	11½″
Width of saddle at rear	1⁷⁄₁₆″	11½″
Width of front leg at body	½″	4″
Width of hind leg at body	²³⁄₃₂″	5¾″
Width of leg at knee	⁵⁄₁₆″	2½″
Width of hoof	¹⁵⁄₃₂″	3¾″
Length of hoof	⅝″	5″
Distance between front hooves	¹³⁄₁₆″	6½″
Distance between hind hooves	¾″	6″

Goat

Illus. 16. This animal is in the prancer position; that is, its two hind feet are on the stand and its front legs are in the air. For a look at the goat in full color, turn to page O of the Color Section.

DIRECTIONS

Using Illus. 17 as a plan, cut out the 11 patterns and glue each pattern to wood of the correct thickness as defined in Table 7. The length of each part should follow the direction of the grain.

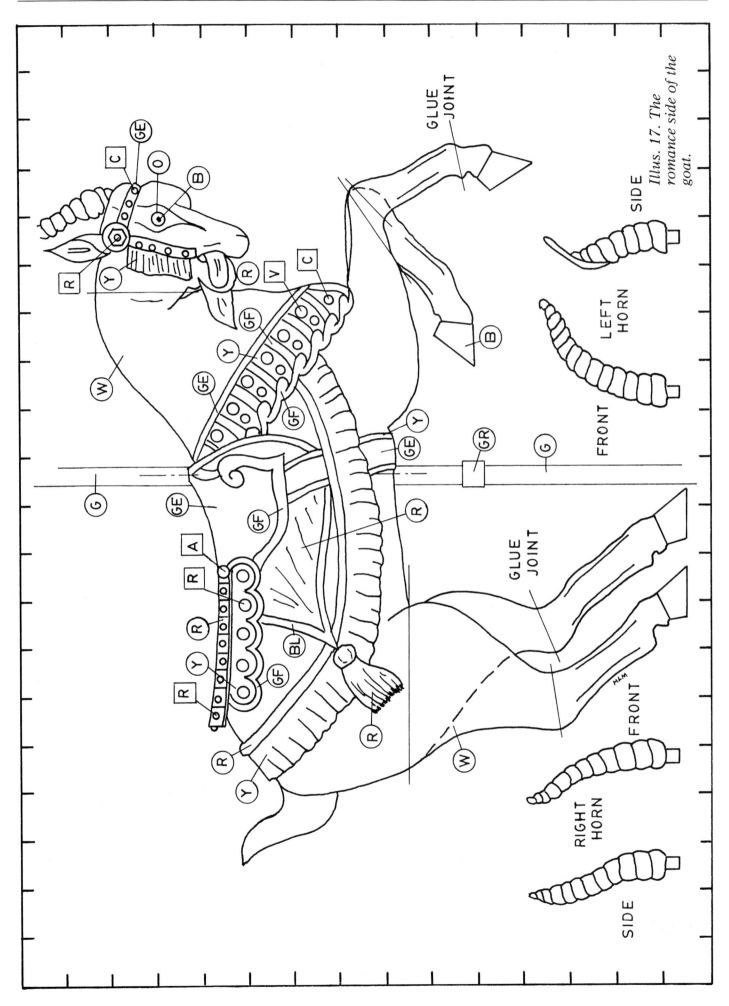

Illus. 17. The romance side of the goat.

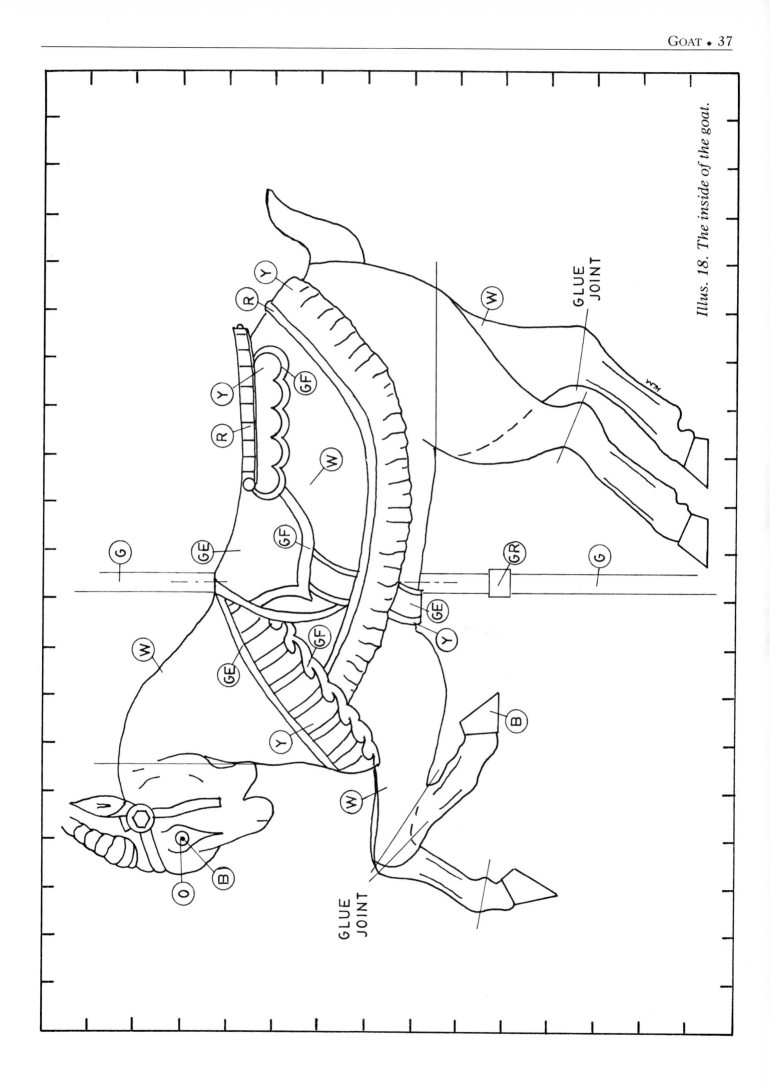

Illus. 18. The inside of the goat.

Table 7   Parts List for the Goat

Part	Length	Width	Thickness
Head	2¼″	1³⁄₁₆″	1″
Body	7¹⁄₁₆″	3⁹⁄₁₆″	1½″
Right Front Leg	1¼″	½″	½″
Right Front Hoof	⅞″	⁷⁄₁₆″	⁷⁄₁₆″
Left Front Leg	2⁵⁄₁₆″	⁹⁄₁₆″	½″
Right Hind Thigh	1¹¹⁄₁₆″	1⅞″	¾″
Right Hind Leg/Hoof	2³⁄₁₆″	⅝″	⁷⁄₁₆″
Left Hind Thigh	1¹¹⁄₁₆″	1⅞″	¾″
Left Hind Leg/Hoof	2³⁄₁₆″	⅝″	⁷⁄₁₆″
Right Horn	1¹¹⁄₁₆″	¹¹⁄₁₆″	⁹⁄₁₆″
Left Horn	1⁹⁄₁₆″	1⅛″	⁹⁄₁₆″

The complete carving block consists of 11 parts, as follow: head, body, right front leg (2 sections), left front leg, right hind leg (2 sections), left hind leg (2 sections) and horns (2). Drill a ³⁄₁₆″ hole through the body before gluing the legs on. Drill two ⅛″ holes ⅛″ deep and ⅜″ apart in the top of the head for the horns (Illus. 17).

Size the end grain of each leg and glue the legs in place. The head should tilt 20° to the right. Cut out the tassel on the rear flank from ⅛″ stock and glue it to the body to provide extra depth.

You can simulate the fleece on the body by using a ⅛″ high-speed cone-shaped steel cutter in a hand-held motor tool. The cloven hooves are pointed at the front. The back of the neck has a flat area about ¼″ wide. The hollow ears are turned slightly to the rear. Refer to Illus. 16–18 and Table 8 to complete the final shapes and details. The approximate carving time is 24 hours.

After carving, paint in accordance with the suggested color scheme or in colors that you prefer. Glue one 4-mm red rhinestone and ten 2-mm crystal rhinestones to the head. Glue fourteen 2-mm red rhinestones, five 4-mm red rhinestones, and an amber rhinestone to the saddle. Glue nine 3-mm violet rhinestones and eight 2-mm crystal rhinestones to the breast band.

Insert a 10¼″ length of ³⁄₁₆″ dowel through the hole in the body so that it extends 4⅜″ above the saddle. Glue it in place and add the footrest (Illus. 5) to the pole. Make a stand and insert the pole of the completed goat into the base.

The following table provides the critical dimensions that you will need when carving a ⅛-scale or full-size model:

Table 8   Critical Dimensions for the Goat

	⅛ Scale	Full Size
Bottom of hoof to top of ear	7″	56″
Width of body at pole	1½″	12″
Width of chest	1⁷⁄₁₆″	11½″
Width of rear flank	1½″	12″
Width of saddle at rear	1³⁄₁₆″	9½″
Width of neck at head	⅞″	7″
Width of neck at body	1⁵⁄₁₆″	10½″
Width of head	1″	8″
Width of nose	⅜″	3″
Distance between eyes	1″	8″
Distance between tips of ears	1¾″	14″
Distance between tips of horns	1⅜″	11″
Width of leg at body (front)	½″	4″
Width of leg at body (hind)	¾″	6″
Width of leg at knee	⁷⁄₁₆″	3½″
Width of leg (thin sections)	⁵⁄₁₆″	2½″
Width of hoof	⁷⁄₁₆″	3½″
Length of hoof	½″	4″
Distance between front hooves	⅝″	5″
Distance between hind hooves	½″	4″
Width of tail	⅜″	3″

King's Horse

Illus. 19. This prancer is covered with armor, and each leaf must be carved separately. It rests on its two hind legs and is supported by the pole. For a look at the king's horse in full color, turn to page O of the Color Section.

DIRECTIONS

Using Illus. 20 as a plan, cut out the eight patterns. Glue each pattern to wood of the correct thickness as defined in Table 9. The length of each part should follow the direction of the grain. Glue the hind legs together at line A–B. Cut the four horseshoes from 1/16″ stock.

Table 9 Parts List for the King's Horse

Part	*Length*	*Width*	*Thickness*
Body	7 3/16″	5 9/16″	1 3/4″
Right Front Leg/Hoof	2 3/16″	9/16″	3/8″
Left Front Leg	1 3/16″	1/2″	3/8″
Left Front Hoof	15/16″	5/8″	7/16″
Right Hind Thigh	1 1/4″	1 7/16″	3/4″
Right Hind Leg/Hoof	2 1/2″	11/16″	7/16″
Left Hind Thigh	1 1/4″	1 7/16″	3/4″
Left Hind Leg/Hoof	2 1/2″	11/16″	7/16″

The complete carving block consists of eight parts, as follow: body, right front leg, left front leg (2 sections), right hind leg (2 sections) and left hind leg (2 sections). Drill a 3/16″ hole through the body for the pole and the 1/8″ hole for the tail before gluing the legs in place. Size the end grain of each part and glue it in place. The head faces straight ahead and has no sideways tilt. The ears are hollow in the rear. Shape the rear of the mane into rounded sections and taper the crown on the top of the head so that the top of the curve is 3/16″ wide. A 5-mm No. 11 veiner gouge will be helpful in carving the individual leaves of the armor. Refer to Illus. 19–21 and Table 10 to complete the final shapes and details. The approximate carving time is 45 hours.

The following table provides the critical dimensions that you will need when carving a 1/8-scale or full-size model:

Table 10 Critical Dimensions for the King's Horse

	1/8 Scale	*Full Size*
Bottom of shoe to top of crown	8 1/8″	65″
Width of body at pole (includes saddle)	1 3/4″	14″
Width of rear flank (includes armor)	1 1/2″	12″
Width of saddle at rear	1 3/8″	11″
Width of neck at body (includes armor)	1 5/16″	10 1/2″
Width of head	1 1/8″	9″
Width of nose	7/16″	3 1/2″
Distance between eyes	3/4″	6″
Distance between tips of ears	7/8″	7″
Width of leg at body (front)	1/2″	4″
Width of leg at body (hind)	3/4″	6″
Width of leg at knee	3/8″	3″
Width of hoof	7/16″	3 1/2″
Length of hoof	5/8″	5″
Distance between front hooves	5/8″	5″
Distance between hind hooves	5/8″	5″

After carving, paint in accordance with the suggested color symbols or in colors more suited to your taste. Glue nine 4-mm crystal

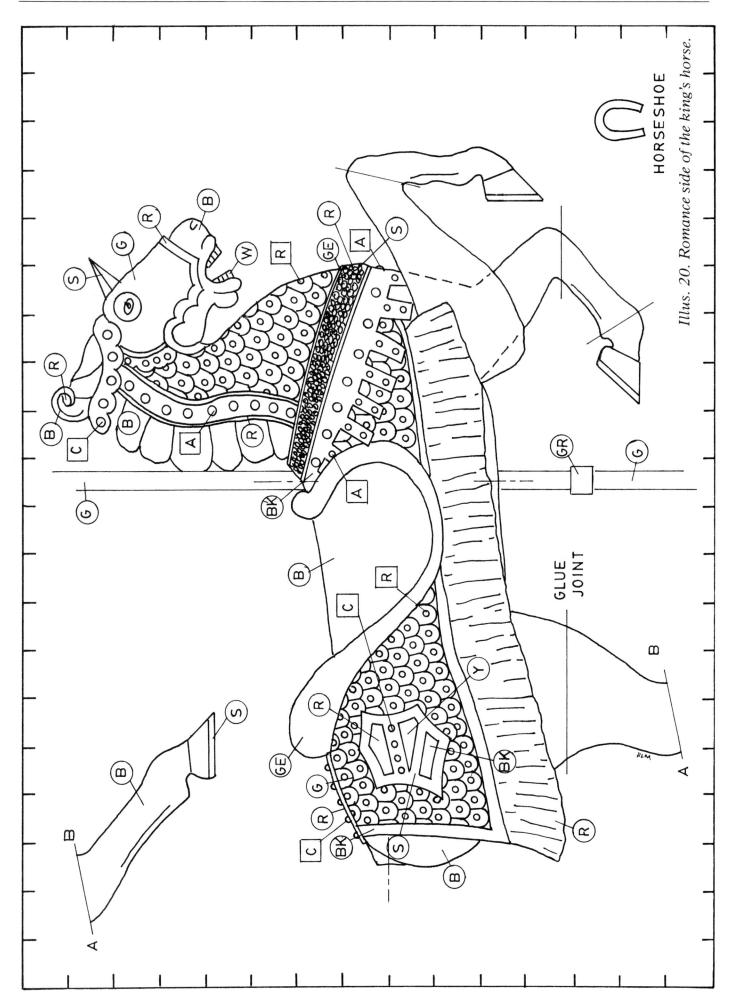

HORSESHOE

Illus. 20. Romance side of the king's horse.

GLUE
JOINT

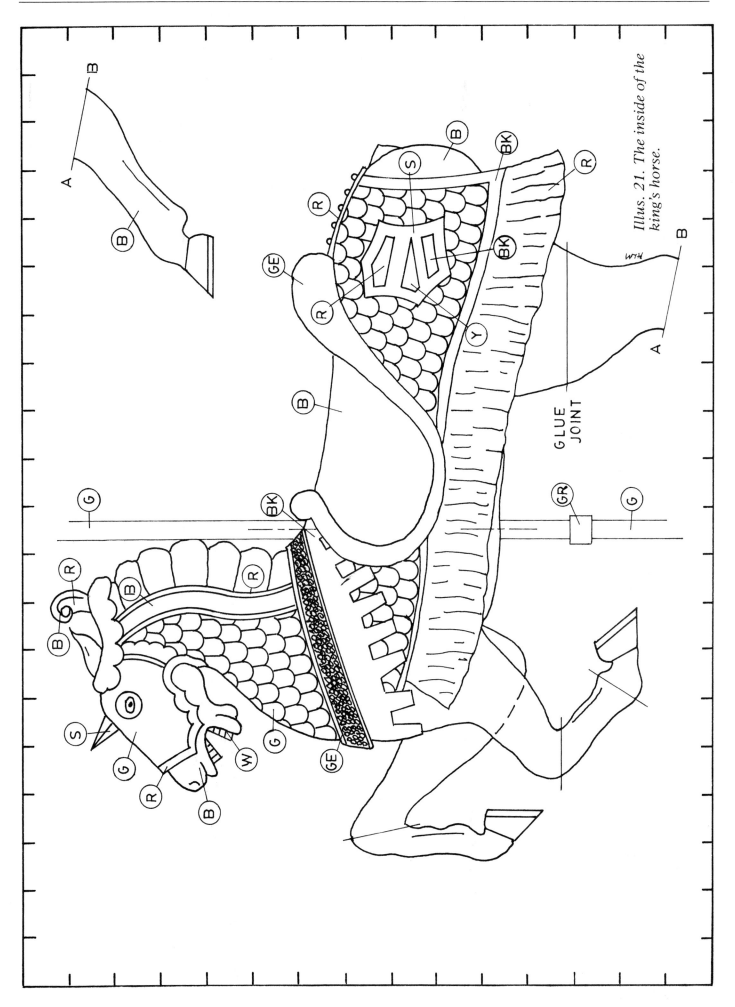

Illus. 21. The inside of the king's horse.

rhinestones to the head, nine 3-mm amber rhinestones to the neck, and sixty-one 2-mm red rhinestones to the neck armor. Glue nine 3-mm amber rhinestones to the breast collar, fifteen 2-mm amber rhinestones to the breast band, and nine 2-mm red rhinestones to the breast armor. Glue fifty-six 2-mm red rhinestones to the rear armor, four 4-mm crystal rhinestones to the shield, and five 4-mm crystal rhinestones to the top of the rear flank. No jewels are on the inside; matching color dots of paint simulate the jewels.

Insert a 10¼″ length of ³⁄₁₆″ dowel through the hole in the body so that ½″ extends below the hind horseshoes. Glue the dowel in place and add the footrest (Illus. 5) to the pole. The tail consists of 95 pieces of heavy-duty black sewing thread 3¼″ long. Make a stand and glue the pole of the completed horse into the hole in the stand.

Stork

Illus. 22. This stork, first carved in 1912, carries the baby on the side of the saddle rather than in its beak. Nevertheless, it is a sentimental favorite. For a look at the stork in full color, turn to page J of the Color Section.

DIRECTIONS

Using Illus. 23 as a plan, cut out the five patterns and glue each pattern to wood of the correct thickness as defined in Table 11. The length of each part should follow the direction of the grain.

The complete carving block consists of five parts, as follow: beak, head/neck, body, right leg, and left leg. Drill a 3/16″ hole through the body for the pole before gluing the neck and legs to the body. Size

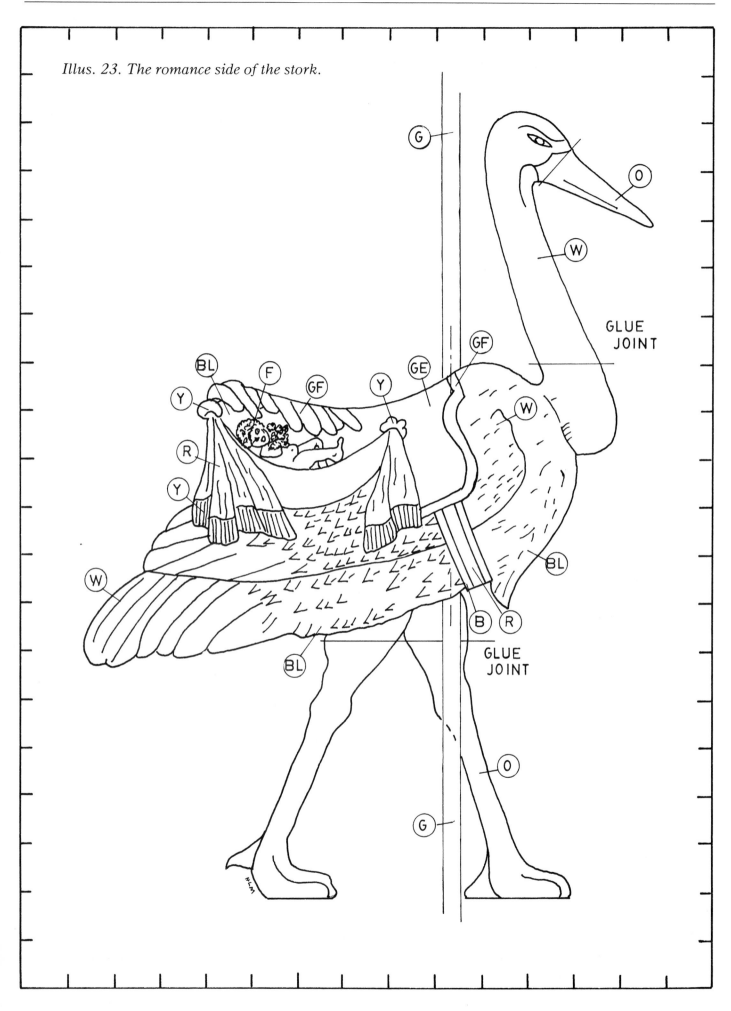

Illus. 23. The romance side of the stork.

GLUE JOINT

GLUE JOINT

Illus. 24. The inside of the stork.

GLUE JOINT

Table 11 Parts List for the Stork

Part	*Length*	*Width*	*Thickness*
Beak	1¼″	½″	⅝″
Head/Neck	2⅝″	1³⁄₁₆″	⅝″
Body	5⅞″	3³⁄₁₆″	1½″
Right Leg	3″	1¼″	½″
Left Leg	3″	1³⁄₁₆″	½″

the end grain of each part and glue it in place. The head faces straight ahead, so there is no sideways tilt. The feathers come to a point in the front. Refer to Illus. 22–24 and Table 12 to complete the final shapes and details. The approximate carving time is 19 hours.

The following table provides the critical dimensions that you will need when carving a ⅛-scale or full-size model:

Table 12 Critical Dimensions for the Stork

	⅛ Scale	*Full Size*
Bottom of foot to top of head	8³⁄₁₆″	65½″
Width of body at pole	1½″	12″
Width of chest	1⁵⁄₁₆″	10½″
Width of saddle at rear	1¼″	10″
Width of head	⅝″	5″
Width of beak at tip	⅛″	1″
Width of neck near head	⁷⁄₁₆″	3½″
Width of neck at base	½″	4″
Width of leg at body	½″	4″
Width of leg at foot	¼″	2″
Width of foot	¹¹⁄₁₆″	5½″
Distance between feet	⅜″	3″
Width of tail	1″	8″

After carving, paint in accordance with the suggested color symbols or in colors which appeal to you that are in keeping with the stork/baby theme. The baby is holding a bunch of multicolored flowers. There are no rhinestones on the stork.

Insert a 10¼″ length of ³⁄₁₆″ dowel through the hole in the body and glue it in place so that 4¼″ extend above the saddle. Make a stand and insert the pole of the completed stork into the base.

Sheik's Horse

GENERAL NOTES

This colorful standing horse, shown in Illus. 25 and 26, belongs to a sheik who has left his scimitar on the horse's side. Its stance seems to be defying motion, but as a member of the carousel it will go around.

DIRECTIONS

Using Illus. 25 as a plan, cut out the nine patterns and glue each pattern to wood of the proper thickness as defined in Table 13. The length of each part should follow the direction of the grain.

Table 13   Parts List for the Sheik's Horse

Part	Length	Width	Thickness
Head	2^{15}/₁₆"	1¼"	1"
Body	6^{13}/₁₆"	3³/₁₆"	1½"
Right Front Leg	1⁷/₁₆"	⅜"	⁹/₁₆"
Right Front Hoof	¹³/₁₆"	½"	⁷/₁₆"
Left Front Leg	2¾"	⅝"	⁹/₁₆"
Right Hind Thigh	1⅛"	¹⁵/₁₆"	¾"
Right Hind Leg	1¹¹/₁₆"	⁹/₁₆"	½"
Left Hind Thigh	1"	1¹/₁₆"	¾"
Left Hind Leg	2¹/₁₆"	⁹/₁₆"	½"

The complete carving block consists of nine parts, as follow: head, body, right front leg (2 sections), left front leg, right hind leg (2 sections), and left hind leg (2 sections). The head is turned 10° to the right. Drill a ³/₁₆" hole through the body for the pole and a ⅛" hole for the tail before gluing the head and legs in place. Size the end grain of each leg part and glue the legs and head in place.

Cut out four horseshoes from ¹/₁₆" stock and glue one to the bottom of each foot. Refer to Illus. 25 and 26 and Table 14 to complete the final shapes and details. The approximate carving time is 35 hours.

Table 14, on page 52, provides the critical dimensions that you will need when carving a ⅛-scale or full-size model.

After carving, paint in colors as suggested or select your own color scheme. Glue a 4-mm red rhinestone to the headband, four 3-mm crystal rhinestones to the face band, four 4-mm crystal rhinestones and four 4-mm red rhinestones to the breast collar, two 3-mm amber rhinestones to the front apron, three 3-mm blue rhinestones to the saddle, three 3-mm red rhinestones to the middle of the sword, five 2-mm red rhinestones to the bottom of the sword, a 2-mm red rhinestone to the top of the sword, and two red and two crystal rhinestones to the top of the rear flank.

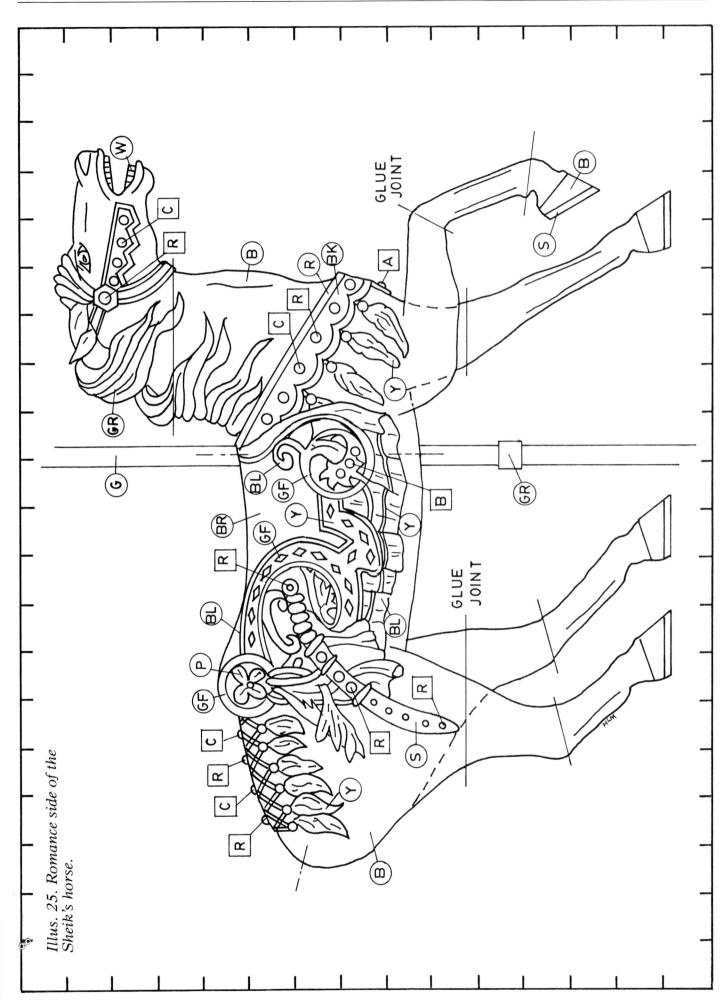

Illus. 25. Romance side of the Sheik's horse.

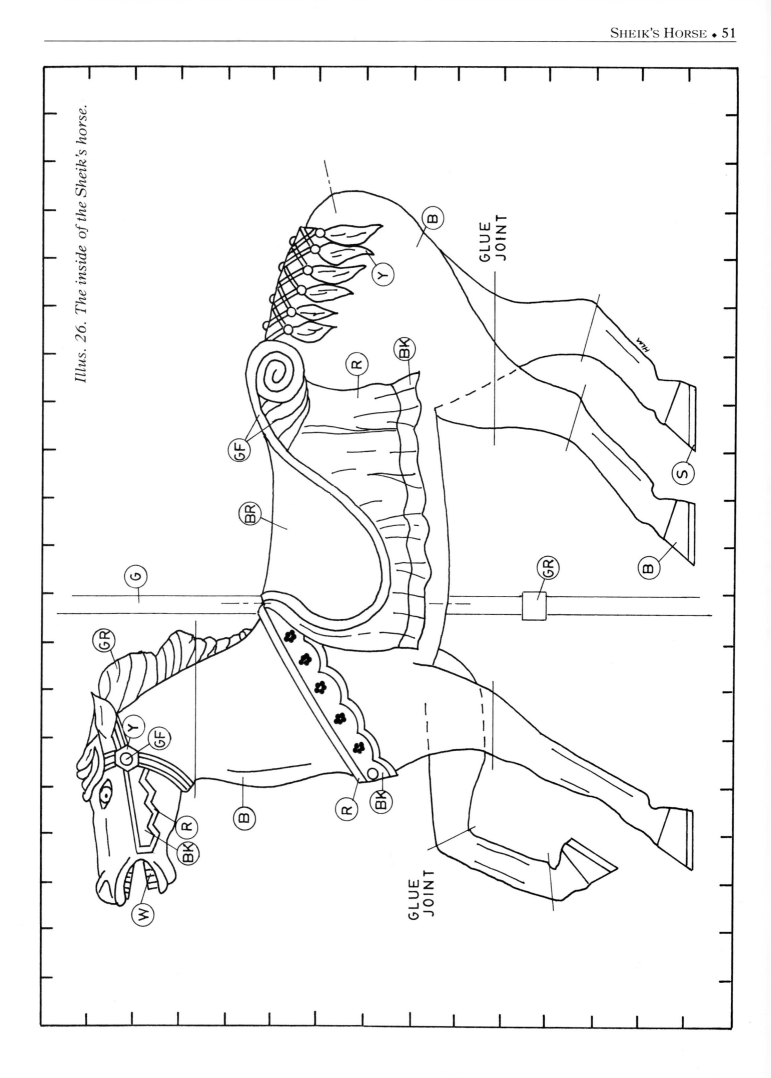

Illus. 26. The inside of the Sheik's horse.

Table 14   Critical Dimensions for the Sheik's Horse

	⅛ Scale	Full Size
Bottom of shoe to top of mane	6¹¹⁄₁₆″	53½″
Width of head (including mane)	1″	8″
Width of head (without mane)	¾″	6″
Width of nose	½″	4″
Distance between eyes	¾″	6″
Distance between tips of ears	¾″	6″
Width of neck at body	1″	8″
Width of body at pole	1⅜″	11″
Width of rear flank	1½″	12″
Width of saddle at rear	1½″	12″
Width of front leg at body	⁹⁄₁₆″	4½″
Width of hind leg at body	¾″	6″
Width of leg at knee	⅜″	3″
Width of hoof	⁷⁄₁₆″	3½″
Length of hoof	⅝″	5″
Distance between front hooves	⅝″	5″
Distance between hind hooves	¹³⁄₁₆″	6½″

Make the tail from approximately sixty 3″ lengths of grey heavy-duty sewing thread. Insert a 10¼″ length of ³⁄₁₆″ dowel through the hole in the body so that 5″ extend above the saddle. Glue it in place and add the footrest (Illus. 5) to the pole. Make a stand and glue the pole of the completed horse to it.

Lion

Illus. 27. The lion—renowned as the King of the Jungle—is longer and wider than any other animal on the carousel. For a look at the lion in full color, turn to page M of the Color Section.

DIRECTIONS

Using Illus. 28 and 29 as a plan, cut out the nine patterns and glue the right hind leg and tail at line A–B. Glue each pattern to wood of the correct thickness as defined in Table 15. The length of each part should follow the direction of the grain.

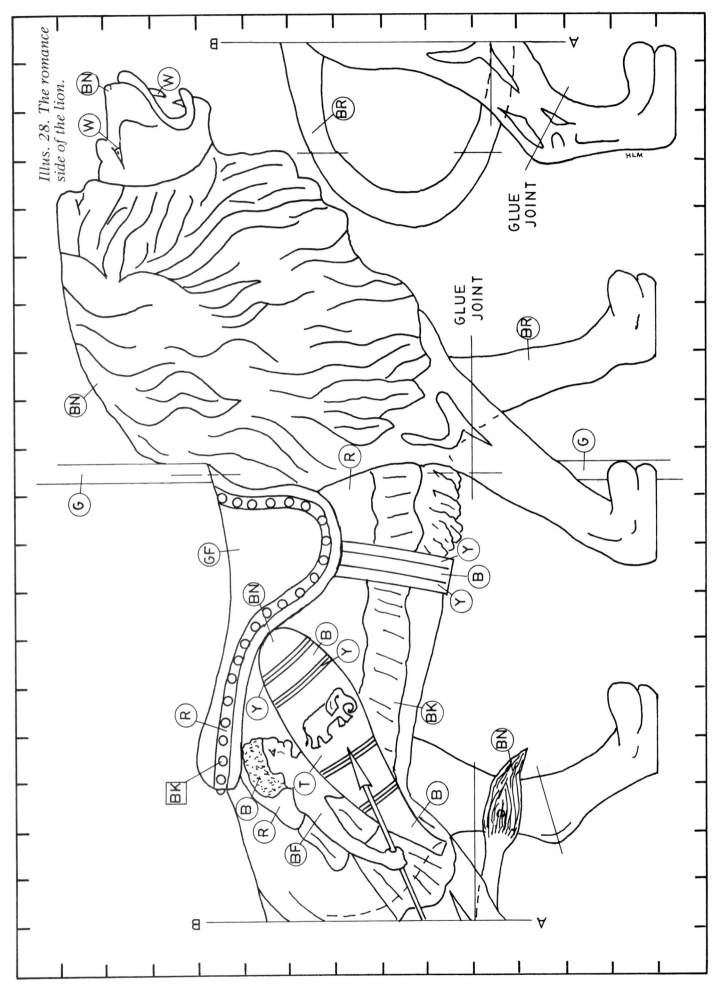

Illus. 28. The romance side of the lion.

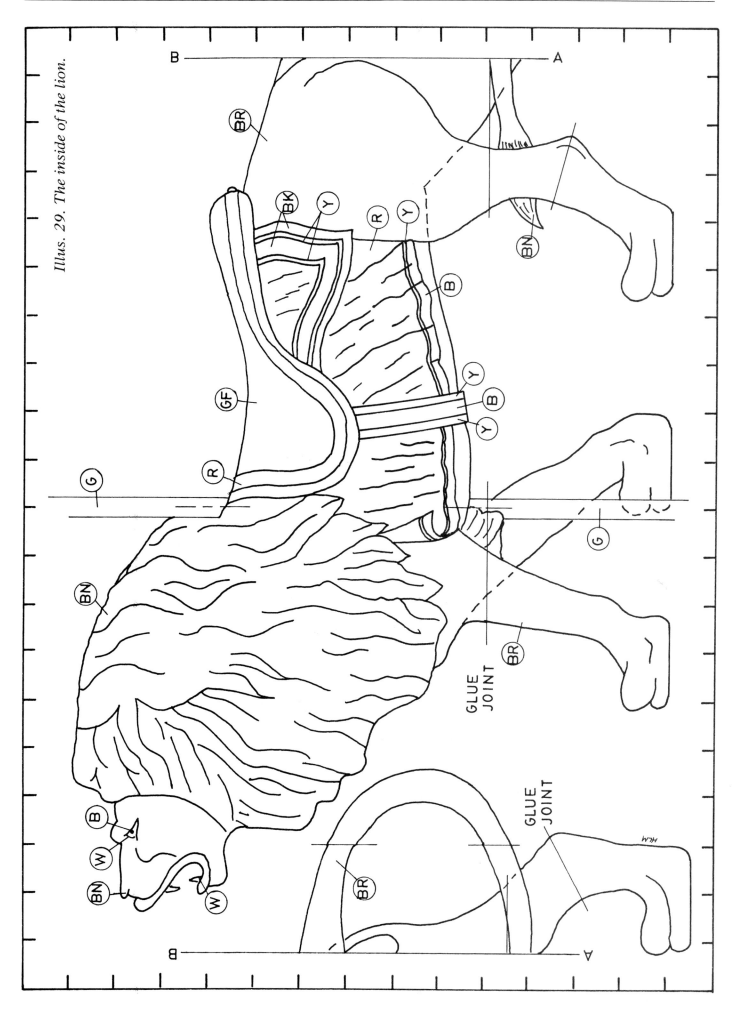

Illus. 29. The inside of the lion.

Table 15   Parts List for the Lion

Part	Length	Width	Thickness
Body	10″	4½″	2½″
Right Front Leg/Foot	2⅝″	1⅛″	¹³⁄₁₆″
Left Front Leg/Foot	2⅜″	1⅛″	¹³⁄₁₆″
Right Hind Thigh	1⅝″	⅞″	⅞″
Right Hind Leg/Foot	1⁹⁄₁₆″	1¼″	¹³⁄₁₆″
Left Hind Thigh	⅞″	⅞″	⅞″
Left Hind Leg/Foot	1¾″	1⅛″	¹³⁄₁₆″
Tail (center)	2″	¹³⁄₁₆″	⁵⁄₁₆″
Tail (end)	3″	⁷⁄₁₆″	⁷⁄₁₆″

The complete carving block consists of nine parts, as follow: body, right front leg, left front leg, right hind leg (2 sections), left hind leg (2 sections), and tail (2 sections). The head is facing straight ahead, so there is no sideways tilt.

Drill a ¹⁄₁₆″ hole in the left hind leg and the end section of the tail to receive the dowel that will support the tail. Drill a ³⁄₁₆″ hole through the body before gluing the legs in place. Size the end grain of each part and glue the legs in place. Glue together the bottom two sections of the tail, and then carve them separately and glue them to the body after you have completely carved and sanded the body.

Glue a ¾″ length of ¹⁄₁₆″ dowel into the tail and leg and glue the tail to the body. You will have to make the ¹⁄₁₆″ dowel since dowels of this diameter are not commercially available.

Refer to Illus. 27–29 and Table 16 to complete the final shapes and details. The carving time is approximately 28 hours.

After carving, paint in accordance with the suggested color symbols or in natural colors. Glue thirty 2-mm dark-blue rhinestones to the saddle. Insert a 10¼″ length of ³⁄₁₆″ dowel through the hole in the body so that ½″ extends below the bottom of the feet. Make a stand and glue the pole of the completed lion to it.

The following table provides the critical dimensions that you will need when carving a ⅛-scale or full-size model:

Table 16 Critical Dimensions for the Lion

	⅛ Scale	*Full Size*
Bottom of foot to top of head	6½″	52″
Width of body at pole	1¾″	14″
Width of rear flank	1¾″	14″
Width of saddle at rear	1 7/16″	11½″
Width of head (including mane)	2½″	20″
Width of face	1⅛″	9″
Width of nose	¾″	6″
Distance between eyes	11/16″	5½″
Distance between tips of ears	2 1/16″	16½″
Width of leg at body (front)	¾″	6″
Width of leg at body (hind)	⅞″	7″
Width of leg at knee (front)	7/16″	3½″
Width of foot	13/16″	6½″
Length of foot	⅞″	7″
Distance between front feet	⅜″	3″
Distance between hind feet	½″	4″
Width of tail at body	⅜″	3″
Width of tail at curve	¼″	2″

Standing White Horse

Illus. 30. Because this horse has three legs on the platform, it is known as a standing horse. For a look at this horse in full color—in particular, its gold mane—turn to page H of the Color Section.

DIRECTIONS

Using Illus. 31 as a plan, cut out the nine patterns and glue each pattern to wood of the correct thickness as defined in Table 17. The length of each part should follow the direction of the grain.

Table 17   Parts List for the Standing White Horse

Part	Length	Width	Thickness
Head	3″	1¼″	⅞″
Body	7¼″	3½″	1½″
Right Front Leg	1⅛″	⁷⁄₁₆″	½″
Right Front Hoof	⅝″	½″	½″
Left Front Leg	2¹⁵⁄₁₆″	¹¹⁄₁₆″	½″
Right Hind Thigh	1″	1″	¾″
Right Hind Leg	1⅞″	½″	½″
Left Hind Thigh	1″	¹⁵⁄₁₆″	¾″
Left Hind Leg	2¹⁄₁₆″	⅝″	½″

The complete carving block consists of nine parts, as follow: head, body, right front leg (2 sections), left front leg, right hind leg (2 sections), and left hind leg (2 sections). Drill a ³⁄₁₆″ hole through the body for the pole and a ⅛″ hole for the tail before gluing the legs to the body. Size the end grain of each part and glue the legs in place. The head tilts 5° sideways to the right. Cut out four horseshoes from ¹⁄₁₆″ stock and glue one to the bottom of each foot. Refer to Illus. 30–32 and Table 18 to complete the final shapes and details. The approximate carving time is 25 hours.

The following table provides the critical dimensions that you will need when carving a ⅛-scale or full-size model:

Table 18   Critical Dimensions for the Standing White Horse

	⅛ Scale	Full Size
Bottom of shoe to top of head	7″	56″
Width of body at pole	1½″	12″
Width of rear flank	1½″	12″
Width of saddle at rear	1½″	12″
Width of head (includes mane)	⅞″	7″
Width of nose	⁷⁄₁₆″	3½″
Distance between eyes	¾″	6″
Distance between tips of ears	⁹⁄₁₆″	4½″
Width of neck at body	¹⁵⁄₁₆″	7½″
Width of leg at body (front)	½″	4″
Width of leg at body (hind)	¾″	6″
Width of leg at knee	¹¹⁄₃₂″	2¾″
Width of hoof	½″	4″
Length of hoof	⅝″	5″
Distance between front hooves	½″	4″
Distance between hind hooves	¹⁵⁄₁₆″	7½″

After carving, paint in accordance with the suggested color symbols. Glue one 4-mm crystal rhinestone and five 2-mm red rhinestones to the head. Glue ten 3-mm dark-blue rhinestones to the edge of the saddle, five 3-mm red rhinestones to the top of the rear

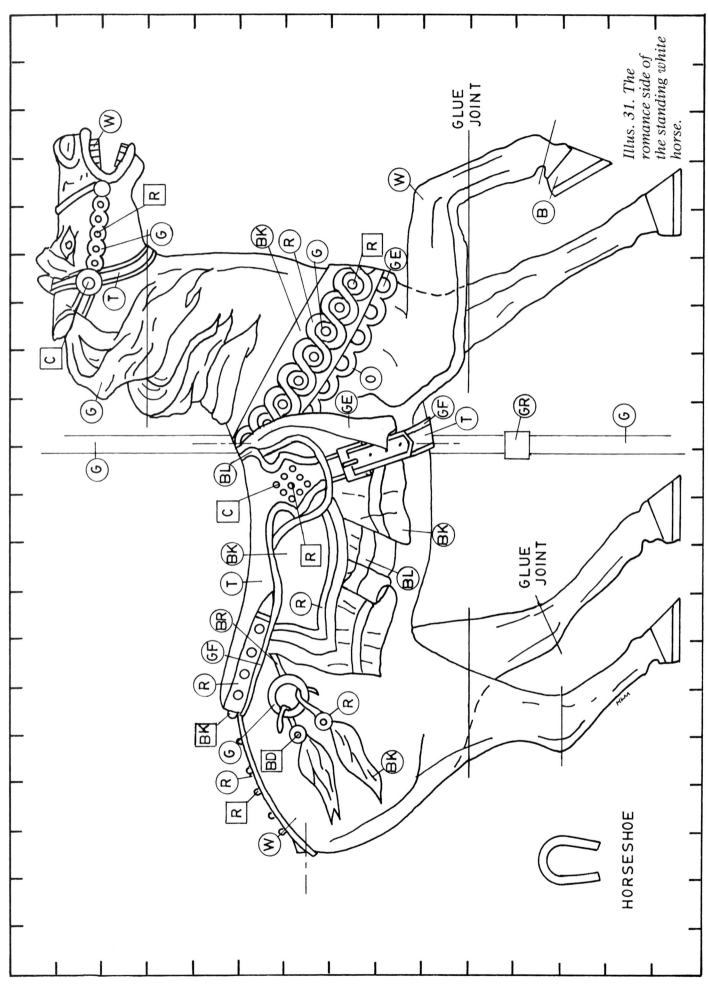

Illus. 31. The romance side of the standing white horse.

HORSESHOE

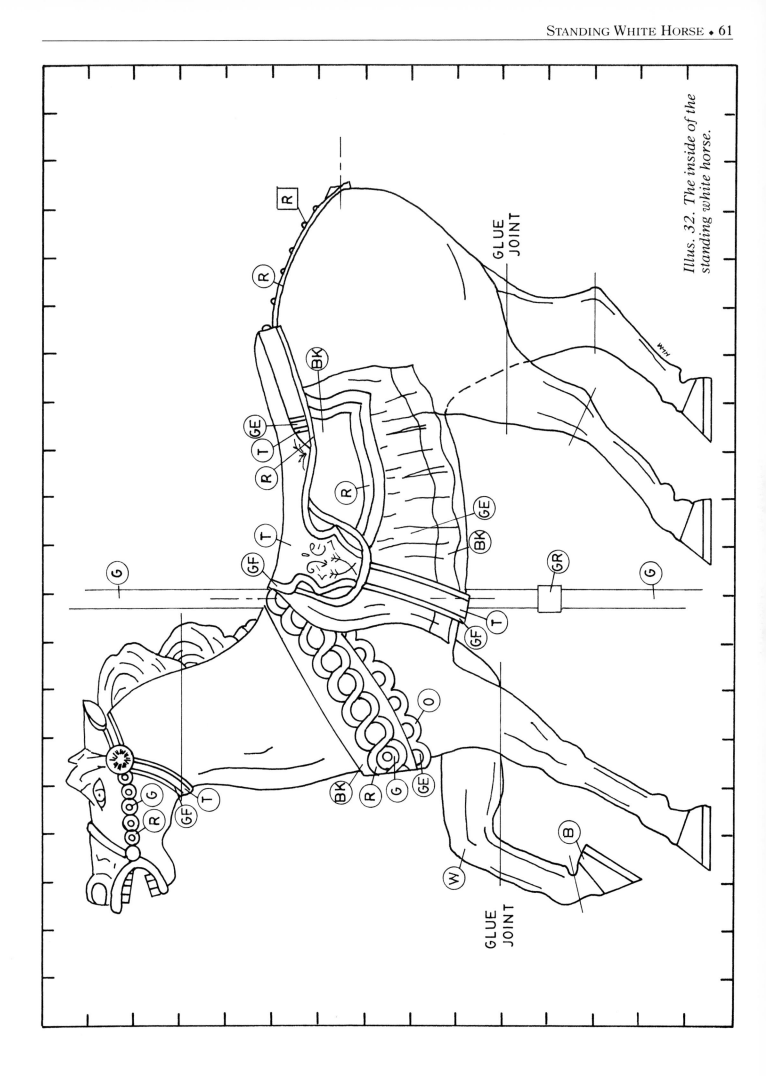

Illus. 32. The inside of the standing white horse.

GLUE JOINT

GLUE JOINT

flank, eleven 3-mm red rhinestones to the breast, eight 2-mm crystal rhinestones and one 2-mm red rhinestone to the side of saddle. Make the tail from 60 pieces of heavy-duty black sewing thread 3″ long.

Insert a 10¼″ length of ³⁄₁₆″ dowel through the hole in the body so that 5″ extend above the saddle. Glue it in place and add the footrest (Illus. 5). Make a stand and glue the pole to it.

Gladiator's Horse

GENERAL NOTES

This gladiator's horse, shown in Illus. 33 and 34, is another elaborately carved animal. It is one of the taller horses on the carousel, and its wide mouth conveys an air of excitement to the rider.

DIRECTIONS

Using Illus. 33 as a plan, cut out the 11 patterns and glue each pattern to wood of the correct thickness as defined in Table 19. You will need Illus. 34 for the complete pattern for the left front leg. The length of each part should follow the direction of the grain.

Table 19   Parts List for the Gladiator's Horse

Part	Length	Width	Thickness
Head	$2^{11}/_{16}''$	$1\frac{1}{2}''$	$1''$
Body	$7''$	$3\frac{3}{4}''$	$1\frac{1}{2}''$
Right Front Leg	$1\frac{3}{8}''$	$\frac{3}{8}''$	$\frac{1}{2}''$
Right Front Hoof	$\frac{7}{8}''$	$\frac{1}{2}''$	$\frac{1}{2}''$
Left Front Thigh	$1\frac{3}{8}''$	$\frac{5}{8}''$	$\frac{1}{2}''$
Left Front Leg	$1\frac{1}{16}''$	$\frac{7}{16}''$	$\frac{1}{2}''$
Left Front Hoof	$\frac{3}{4}''$	$\frac{7}{16}''$	$\frac{1}{2}''$
Right Hind Thigh	$1\frac{7}{16}''$	$1\frac{1}{2}''$	$\frac{3}{4}''$
Right Hind Leg	$2\frac{1}{8}''$	$\frac{5}{8}''$	$\frac{1}{2}''$
Left Hind Thigh	$1\frac{3}{8}''$	$1\frac{7}{8}''$	$\frac{3}{4}''$
Left Hind Leg	$2\frac{1}{4}''$	$\frac{5}{8}''$	$\frac{1}{2}''$

The complete carving block consists of 11 parts, as follow: head, body, right front leg (2 sections), left front leg (3 sections), right hind leg (2 sections) and left hind leg (2 sections). The head is turned 10° to the right.

Drill a $\frac{3}{16}''$ hole through the body for the pole and a $\frac{1}{8}''$ hole for the tail. Size the end grain of each leg part and glue the legs and head to the body. Cut out the gladiator and shield from $\frac{3}{8}''$ stock and glue them to the body. The finished head should extend $\frac{3}{8}''$ beyond the saddle, and the front of the shield should tilt towards the horse. Cut out four horseshoes from $\frac{1}{16}''$ stock and glue one to the bottom of each foot. Refer to Illus. 33 and 34 and Table 20 for the finished carving details. The approximate carving time is 35 hours.

Table 20, on page 66, provides the critical dimensions that you will need when carving a $\frac{1}{8}$-scale or full-size model.

After carving, paint as suggested or develop your own color scheme. Glue one 4-mm red rhinestone to the headband, thirteen 3-mm amber rhinestones and nine 2-mm red rhinestones to the breast

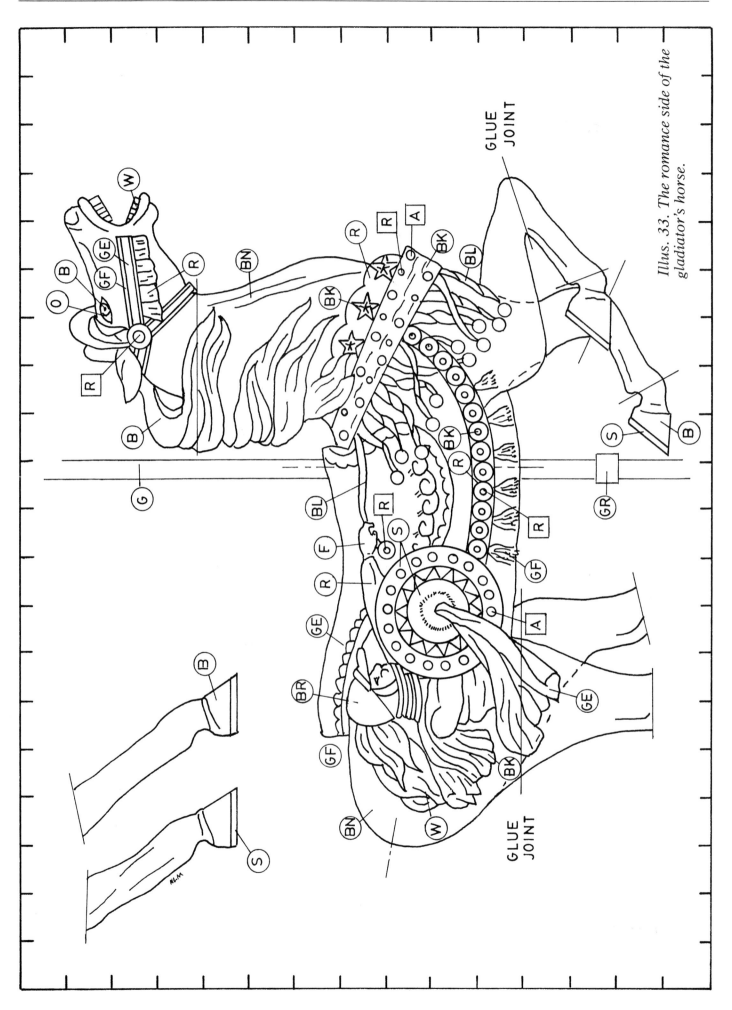

Illus. 33. The romance side of the gladiator's horse.

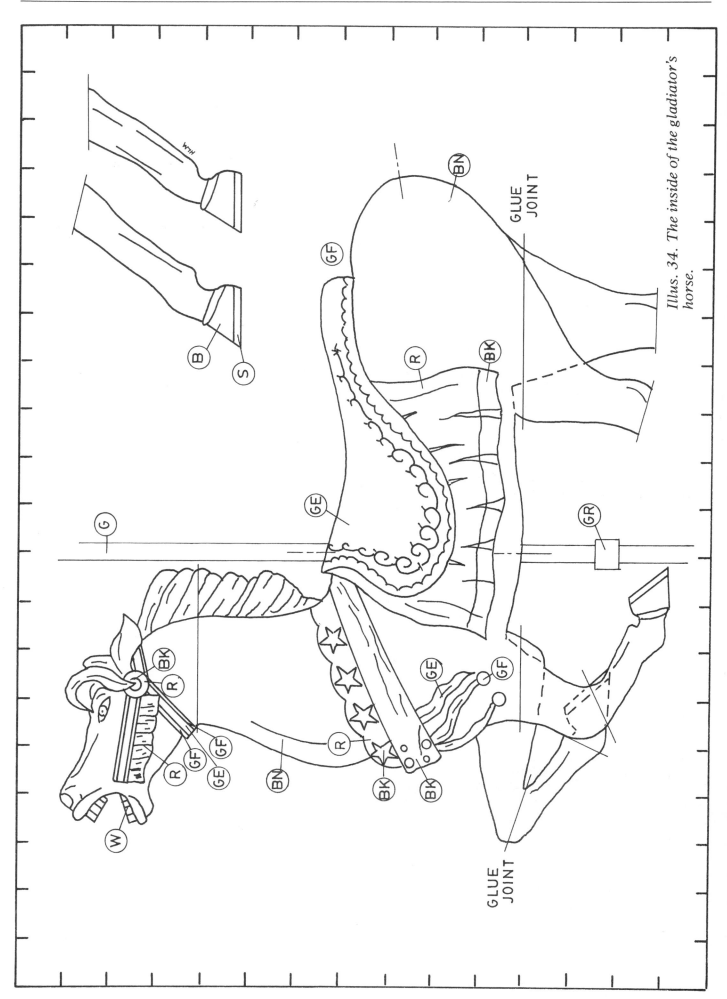

Illus. 34. The inside of the gladiator's horse.

collar, fourteen 2-mm red rhinestones to the side, and sixteen 4-mm amber rhinestones to the shield. The tail consists of approximately 60 strands, each 3″ long, of black heavy-duty sewing thread.

Insert a 10¼″ length of ³⁄₁₆″ dowel through the hole in the body and glue it in place so that 4⅛″ extend above the saddle. Put the footrest (Illus. 5) on the pole and glue it so that the top is ¹³⁄₁₆″ beneath the belly of the horse. Make a stand and glue the pole of the completed horse to it.

Table 20   Critical Dimensions for the Gladiator's Horse

	⅛ Scale	Full Size
Bottom of shoe to top of mane	8″	64″
Width of head (including mane)	1″	8″
Width of mouth	⁷⁄₁₆″	3½″
Width of nose	½″	4″
Distance between eyes	²⁷⁄₃₂″	6¾″
Distance between tips of ears	¾″	6″
Width of neck at body	⅞″	7″
Width of neck at head	¾″	6″
Width of body at pole	1⅜″	11″
Width of rear flank	1½″	12″
Width of saddle at rear	1½″	12″
Width of front leg at body	½″	4″
Width of hind leg at body	¾″	6″
Width of leg at knee	⅜″	3″
Width of hoof	½″	4″
Length of hoof	⅝″	5″
Distance between front hooves	¾″	6″
Distance between hind hooves	⅞″	7″

Tiger

Illus. 35. The inside of the tiger is carved in much more detail than is typical of most of the other animals. Its mane is not anatomically correct, but was added for effect. For a look at the tiger in full color, turn to page F of the Color Section.

DIRECTIONS

Using Illus. 36 as a plan, cut out the eight patterns and glue each pattern to wood of the correct thickness as defined in Table 21. The length of each part should follow the direction of the grain.

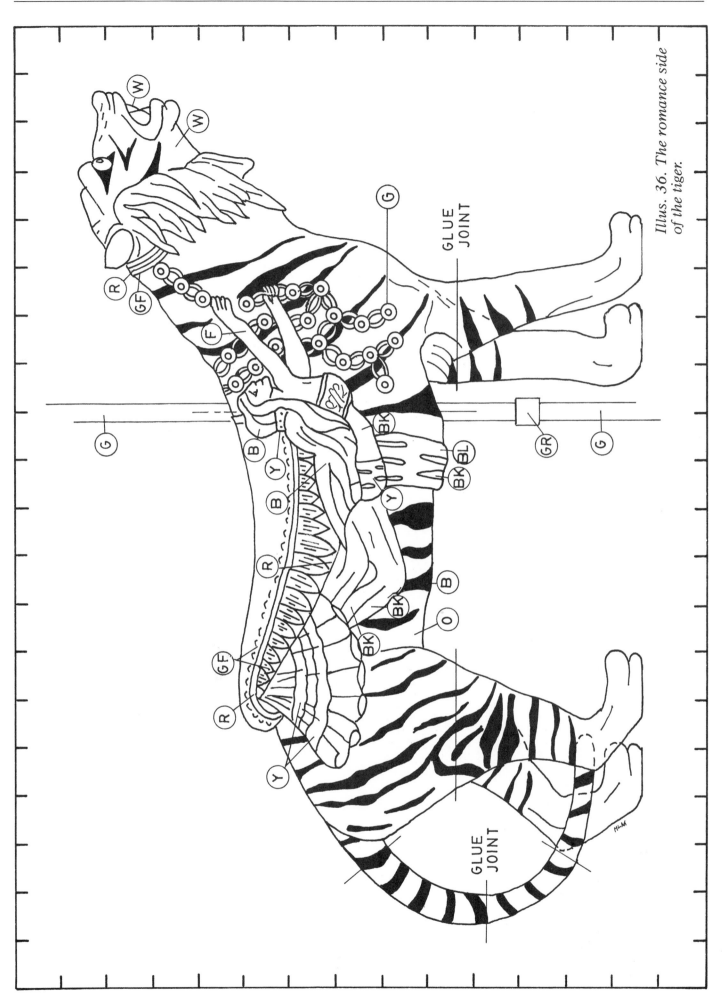

Illus. 36. The romance side of the tiger.

GLUE JOINT

GLUE JOINT

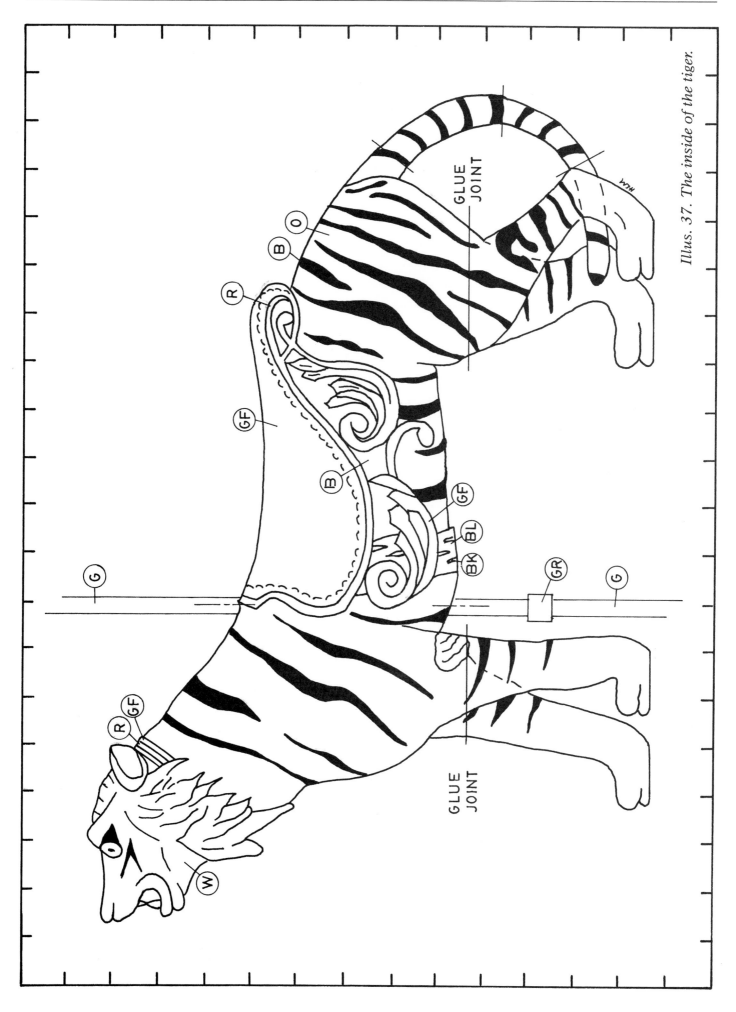

Illus. 37. The inside of the tiger.

Table 21   Parts List for the Tiger

Part	Length	Width	Thickness
Body	8⅛"	4¹⁄₁₆"	1¹¹⁄₁₆"
Right Front Leg	2⅜"	⅞"	⅝"
Left Front Leg	2"	⅞"	⅝"
Right Hind Leg	2"	1⁵⁄₁₆"	¹³⁄₁₆"
Left Hind Leg	2"	2"	¹³⁄₁₆"
Tail (top)	1½"	½"	⅜"
Tail (center)	1³⁄₁₆"	⁷⁄₁₆"	⁵⁄₁₆"
Tail (bottom)	1⅜"	⅜"	⁵⁄₁₆"

The complete carving block consists of eight parts, as follow: body, right front leg, left front leg, right hind leg, left hind leg, and tail (3 sections). The head faces straight ahead, so there is no sideways tilt.

Drill a ³⁄₁₆" hole through the body before gluing the legs in place. Size the end grain of each part and glue the legs to the body. Glue the bottom three sections of the tail together, carve them separately, and glue them to the body and left hind leg after you have completely carved and sanded the body. Refer to Illus. 35–37 and Table 22 to complete the final shapes and details. The carving time is approximately 24 hours.

The following table provides the critical dimensions that you will need when carving a ⅛-scale or full-size model:

Table 22   Critical Dimensions for the Tiger

	⅛ Scale	Full Size
Bottom of foot to top of head	6⅛"	49"
Width of body at pole	1¹¹⁄₁₆"	13½"
Width of rear flank	1⅜"	11"
Width of saddle at rear	1¹¹⁄₁₆"	13½"
Width of head	1¼"	10"
Width of nose	¹¹⁄₁₆"	5½"
Distance between eyes	⅞"	7"
Distance between tips of ears	1¼"	10"
Width of neck below head	1¼"	10"
Width of leg at body (front)	⅝"	5"
Width of leg at body (hind)	¹³⁄₁₆"	6½"
Width of leg at ankle	⁷⁄₁₆"	3½"
Width of foot	⅝"	5"
Length of foot	⅝"	5"
Distance between front feet	⁹⁄₁₆"	4½"
Distance between hind feet	¼"	2"
Width of tail at body	⅜"	3"
Width of tail at bend	¼"	2"

After carving, paint in accordance with the suggested color symbols or according to your preference. Glue twenty-one 3-mm green rhinestones to the side and neck. Insert a 10¼″ length of ³⁄₁₆″ dowel through the body so that ½″ extends below the bottom of the feet. Glue it in place and add the footrest (Illus. 5) to the pole. Make a stand and put the pole of the completed tiger in the hole in the stand.

Camel

Illus. 38. The humps on the camel constitute the seat for the rider; there is no other saddle on this animal. For a look at the camel in full color, turn to page N of the Color Section.

DIRECTIONS

Using Illus. 39 as a plan, cut out the nine patterns and glue each pattern to wood of the correct thickness as defined in Table 23. Refer to Illus. 40 for the complete pattern for the left front leg. The length of each part should follow the direction of the grain.

The complete carving block consists of nine parts, as follow: body, right front leg, left front leg (2 sections), right hind leg (2 sections),

Table 23 Parts List for the Camel

Part	*Length*	*Width*	*Thickness*
Body	7 7/16″	3 1/16″	1 5/8″
Right Front Leg/Foot	2 13/16″	13/16″	7/16″
Left Front Thigh	1 1/8″	11/16″	7/16″
Left Front Leg/Foot	1 7/8″	11/16″	1/2″
Right Hind Thigh	1 3/8″	7/8″	3/4″
Right Hind Leg/Foot	1 15/16″	13/16″	1/2″
Left Hind Thigh	1 1/16″	7/8″	3/4″
Left Hind Leg/Foot	2 1/4″	3/4″	1/2″
Tail	2 3/4″	1/2″	1/4″

left hind leg (2 sections), and tail. Drill a 3/16″ hole through the center of the front hump for the pole. Size the end grain of each part and glue the legs in place. The head faces straight ahead, so there is no sideways tilt.

Carve the rings separately, and interweave and glue them to the side above the tassels. Cut out from 1/8″ stock the three side tassels and glue them on the romance side to provide added depth. There are 16 leaves on the front hump and 12 on the rear hump. Each foot has only two toes. Glue the tail to the body and the right hind leg after you have completely carved and sanded the body. Refer to Illus. 38–40 and Table 24 to complete the final shapes and details. The approximate carving time is 20 hours.

The following table provides the critical dimensions that you will need when carving a 1/8-scale or full-size model:

Table 24 Critical Dimensions for the Camel

	1/8 Scale	*Full Size*
Bottom of foot to top of head	5 11/16″	45 1/2″
Width of body at pole	1 5/8″	13″
Width of rear flank	1 1/2″	12″
Width of saddle at rear	1 5/8″	13″
Width of head	3/4″	6″
Width of nose	3/8″	3″
Distance between tips of ears	1 1/32″	8 1/4″
Width of neck at body	1 1/8″	9″
Width of neck at head	3/4″	6″
Width of leg at body (front)	7/16″	3 1/2″
Width of leg at body (hind)	3/4″	6″
Width of leg at knee	1/2″	4″
Width of leg (thin area)	7/32″	1 3/4″
Width of foot	1/2″	4″
Length of foot	3/4″	6″
Distance between front feet	3/4″	6″
Distance between hind feet	11/16″	5 1/2″
Width of tail	1/8″	1″

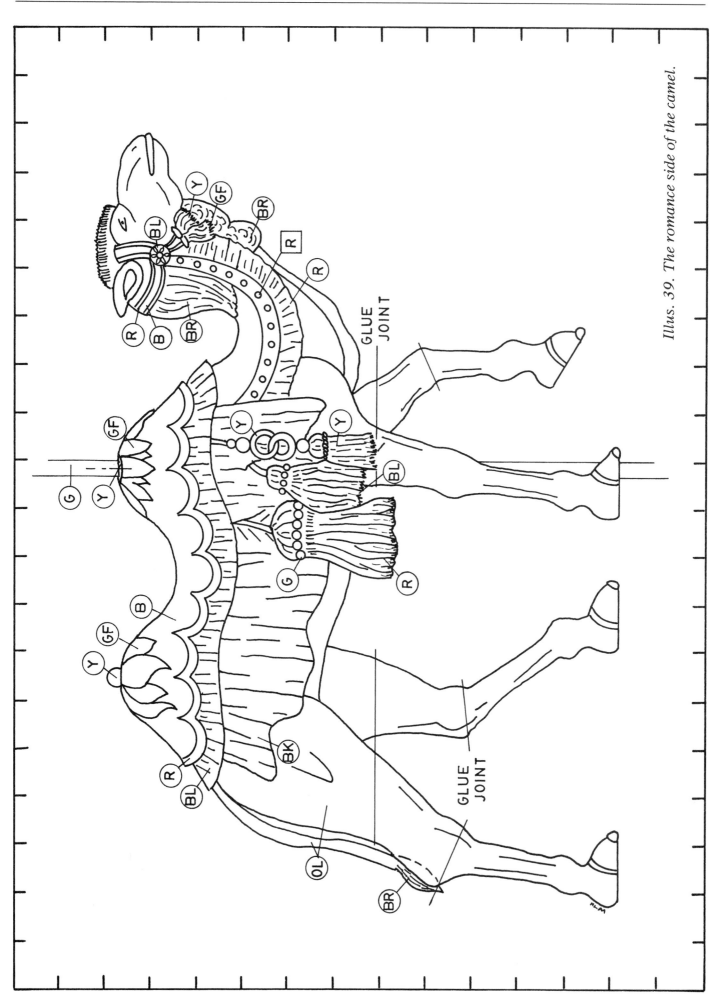

Illus. 39. The romance side of the camel.

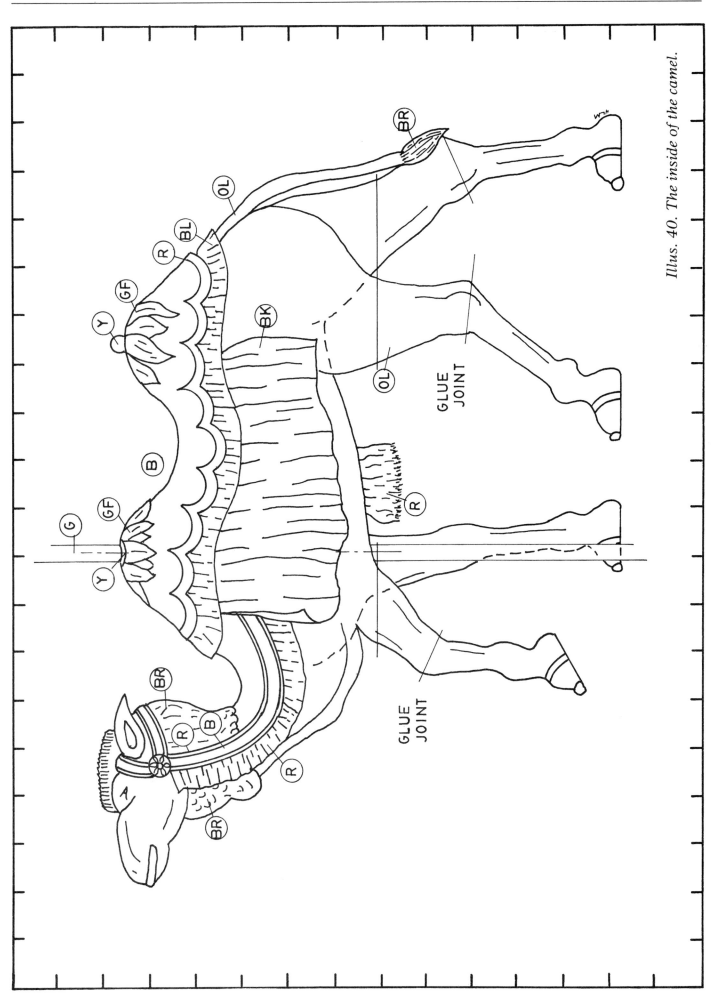

Illus. 40. The inside of the camel.

After carving, paint in accordance with the suggested color symbols or select colors you find appealing. Glue twelve 2-mm red rhinestones to the neckband. Insert a 10¼″ length of ³⁄₁₆″ dowel through the hole in the body and glue it so that 4¼″ extend above the front hump. Make a stand and glue the pole of the completed camel to it.

Horse with Green Blanket

GENERAL NOTES

This horse, shown in Illus. 41 and 42, has no unusual distinctive features, but is typical of the many colorful animals one thinks of when the word carousel is mentioned.

DIRECTIONS

Using Illus. 41 as a plan, cut out the nine patterns and glue each pattern to wood of the correct thickness as defined in Table 25. The length of each part should follow the direction of the grain.

Table 25 Parts List for the Horse with Green Blanket

Part	*Length*	*Width*	*Thickness*
Body	$8\frac{3}{16}''$	$4''$	$1\frac{1}{2}''$
Right Front Leg	$1\frac{7}{16}''$	$\frac{7}{16}''$	$\frac{1}{2}''$
Right Front Hoof	$\frac{11}{16}''$	$\frac{7}{16}''$	$\frac{1}{2}''$
Left Front Leg	$2\frac{15}{16}''$	$\frac{11}{16}''$	$\frac{1}{2}''$
Right Hind Thigh	$1\frac{1}{8}''$	$\frac{15}{16}''$	$\frac{3}{4}''$
Right Hind Leg	$2\frac{3}{16}''$	$\frac{5}{8}''$	$\frac{1}{2}''$
Left Hind Thigh	$1\frac{1}{2}''$	$\frac{15}{16}''$	$\frac{3}{4}''$
Left Hind Leg	$1\frac{5}{8}''$	$\frac{11}{16}''$	$\frac{1}{2}''$
Left Hind Hoof	$\frac{13}{16}''$	$\frac{1}{2}''$	$\frac{1}{2}''$

The complete carving block consists of nine parts, as follow: body, right front leg (2 sections), left front leg, right hind leg (2 sections), and left hind leg (3 sections). There is no tilt to the head.

Drill a $\frac{3}{16}''$ hole through the body for the pole and a $\frac{1}{8}''$ hole for the tail before gluing the legs to the body. Size the end grain of each leg part and glue the legs to the body. Cut out four horseshoes from $\frac{1}{16}''$ stock and glue one to the bottom of each foot. Refer to Illus. 41 and 42 and Table 26 when carving the final shapes and details. The approximate carving time is 20 hours.

Table 26, on page 80, provides the critical dimensions that you will need when carving a $\frac{1}{8}$-scale or full-size horse.

After carving, follow the suggested color scheme for painting or select your own colors. Glue six 3-mm red rhinestones and five 3-mm crystal rhinestones to the breast collar, one 3-mm red rhinestone and eight 3-mm crystal rhinestones to the side of the saddle, seven 2-mm green rhinestones to the rear of the saddle, and three 3-mm red rhinestones to the top of the rear flank. The tail is made of approximately 60 lengths of black heavy-duty sewing thread, each piece $2\frac{1}{2}''$ long.

Insert a $10\frac{1}{4}''$ length of $\frac{3}{16}''$ dowel through the hole in the body so

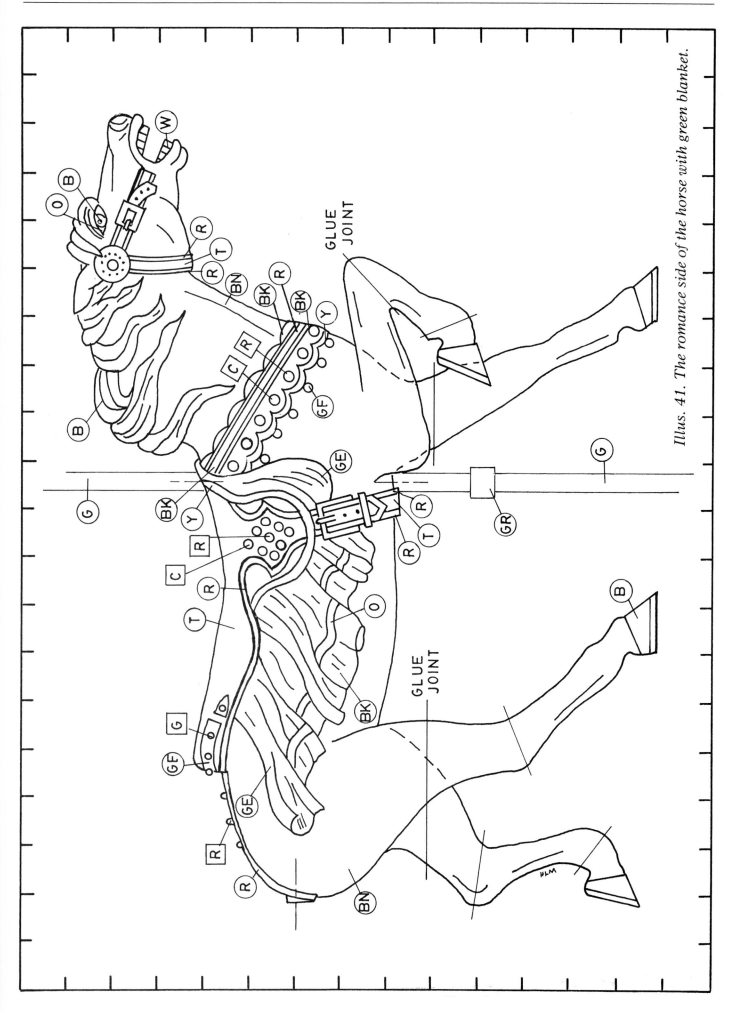

Illus. 41. The romance side of the horse with green blanket.

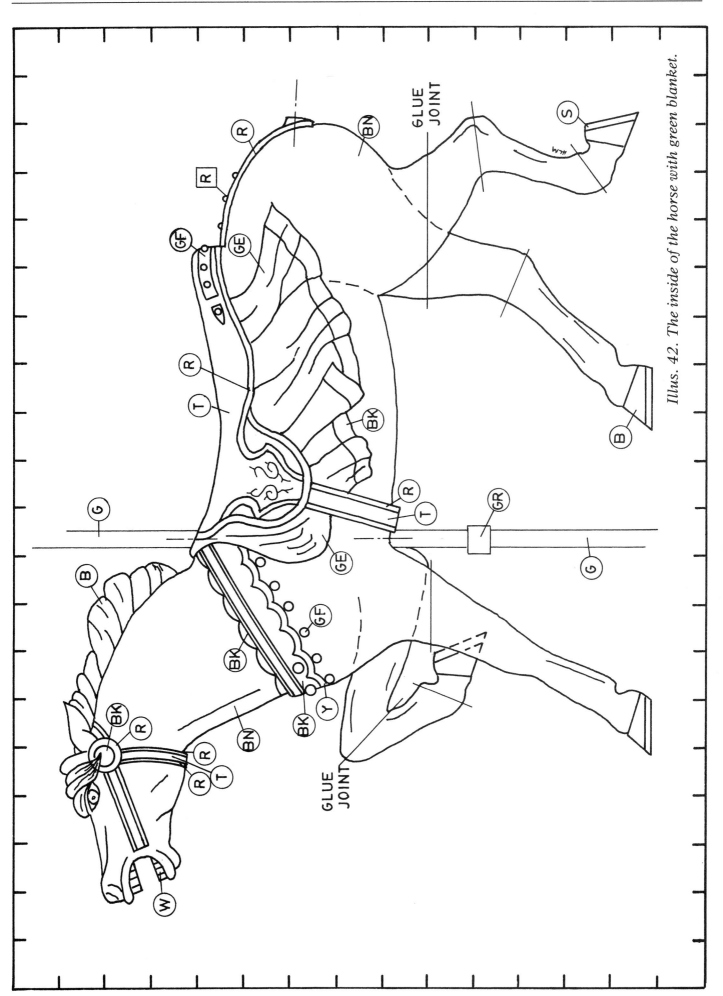

Illus. 42. The inside of the horse with green blanket.

that 4⅞" extend above the saddle. Glue it in place and add the footrest (Illus. 5). Make a stand and glue the pole of the completed horse to it.

Table 26   Critical Dimensions for the Horse with Green Blanket

	⅛ Scale	Full Size
Bottom of shoe to top of mane	6⁷⁄₁₆"	51½"
Width of head (including mane)	1"	8"
Width of nose	¹⁵⁄₃₂"	3¾"
Distance between eyes	⅞"	7"
Distance between tips of ears	⅝"	5"
Width of neck at body	1"	8"
Width of neck at head	¾"	6"
Width of body at pole	1½"	12"
Width of rear flank	1½"	12"
Width of saddle at rear	1½"	12"
Width of front leg at body	½"	4"
Width of hind leg at body	¾"	6"
Width of leg at knee	⁵⁄₁₆"	2½"
Width of hoof	⁷⁄₁₆"	3½"
Length of hoof	⅝"	5"
Distance between front hooves	⅝"	5"
Distance between hind hooves	¹³⁄₁₆"	6½"

Brown Horse

GENERAL NOTES

This horse, shown in Illus. 43 and 44, is wearing roses in its mane and gives the impression that it's waiting impatiently for a rider.

DIRECTIONS

Using Illus. 43 as a plan, cut out the ten patterns and glue each pattern to wood of the correct thickness as stated in Table 27. You will have to refer to Illus. 44 for the complete pattern for the left front leg. The length of each part should follow the direction of the grain.

Table 27   Parts List for the Brown Horse

Part	Length	Width	Thickness
Head	2⁷⁄₁₆″	1⅛″	⅞″
Body	6⁵⁄₁₆″	4⅛″	1⅜″
Right Front Leg	1⁵⁄₁₆″	⅜″	½″
Right Front Hoof	¾″	⅜″	⁷⁄₁₆″
Left Front Leg	3″	¹⁵⁄₁₆″	½″
Right Hind Thigh	2″	1⁵⁄₁₆″	¹¹⁄₁₆″
Right Hind Leg	1⅝″	⁷⁄₁₆″	⁷⁄₁₆″
Left Hind Thigh	2″	1⅛″	¹¹⁄₁₆″
Left Hind Leg	1⁵⁄₁₆″	⅜″	½″
Left Hind Hoof	½″	⁷⁄₁₆″	⁷⁄₁₆″

The complete carving block consists of ten parts, as follow: head, body, right front leg (2 sections), left front leg, right hind leg (2 sections), and left hind leg (3 sections). Drill a ³⁄₁₆″ hole through the body for the pole and a ⅛″ hole for the tail. Size the end grain of each part and glue the head and legs to the body. Cut out four horseshoes from ¹⁄₁₆″ stock and glue one to the bottom of each foot. The head tilts 33° to the right. Refer to Illus. 43 and 44 and Table 28 to carve the final shapes and details. The approximate carving time is 20 hours.

Table 28, on page 84, provides the critical dimensions that you will need when carving a ⅛-scale or full-size carving.

After carving, paint as suggested by the color scheme or according to your own preferences. Glue ten 3-mm red rhinestones to the front apron (each of these rhinestones should be set in the center of a white, five-pointed star), five 4-mm crystal rhinestones to the saddle blanket, and three 3-mm crystal rhinestones to the top of the rear flank. Make the tail from approximately 60 lengths of light-brown sewing thread. Each strand should be 2½″ long.

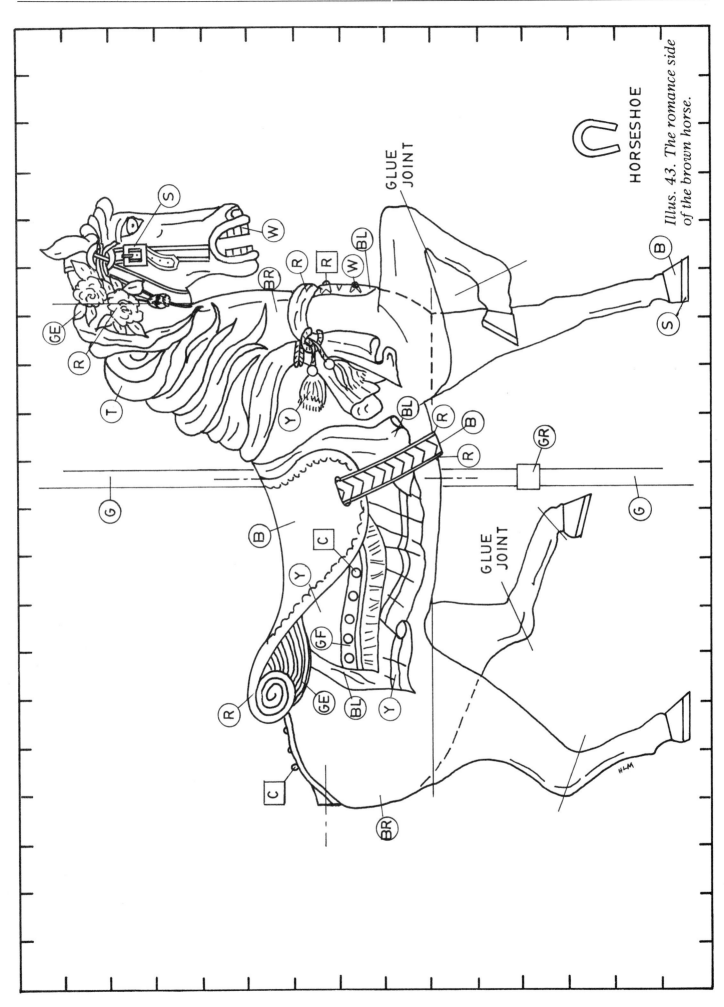

HORSESHOE

Illus. 43. The romance side of the brown horse.

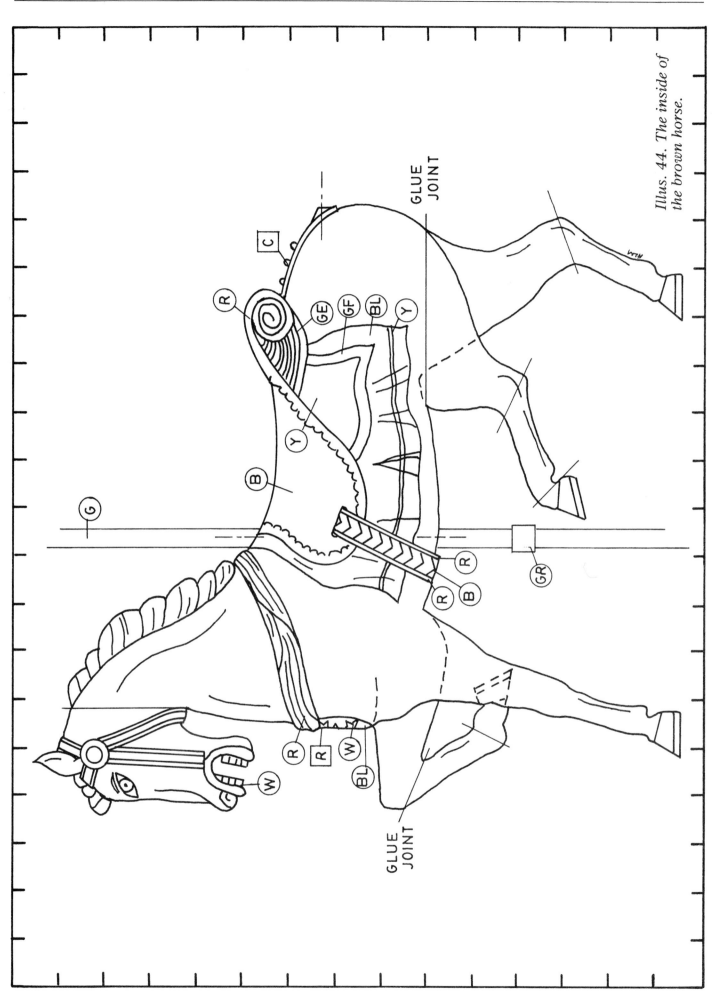

Illus. 44. The inside of the brown horse.

Insert a 10¼″ length of 3⁄16″ dowel through the body and glue it in place so that 5⅛″ extend above the saddle. Add a footrest (Illus. 5) to the pole. Make a stand and glue the pole of the completed carving to it.

Table 28 Critical Dimensions for the Brown Horse

	⅛ Scale	*Full Size*
Bottom of shoe to top of ear	7″	56″
Width of head (including mane)	⅞″	7″
Width of mouth	5⁄16″	2½″
Width of nose	7⁄16″	3½″
Distance between eyes	¾″	6″
Distance between tips of ears	19⁄32″	4¾″
Width of neck at ribbon	1⅛″	9″
Width of body at pole	1⅜″	11″
Width of rear flank	1 5⁄16″	10½″
Width of saddle at rear	1⅜″	11″
Width of front leg at body	½″	4″
Width of hind leg at body	11⁄16″	5½″
Width of leg at knee	⅜″	3″
Width of hoof	7⁄16″	3½″
Length of hoof	½″	4″
Distance between front hooves	¾″	6″
Distance between hind hooves	⅝″	5″

Reindeer

Illus. 45. The highlight of this sleek animal is its majestic rack. On its rear flank is the head of a hunting dog. For a look at the reindeer in full color, turn to page P of the Color Section.

DIRECTIONS

Using Illus. 46 as a plan, cut out the eight patterns and glue each pattern to wood of the correct thickness as defined in Table 29. You will have to refer to Illus. 47 for a complete pattern for the left front leg. The length of each part should follow the direction of the grain.

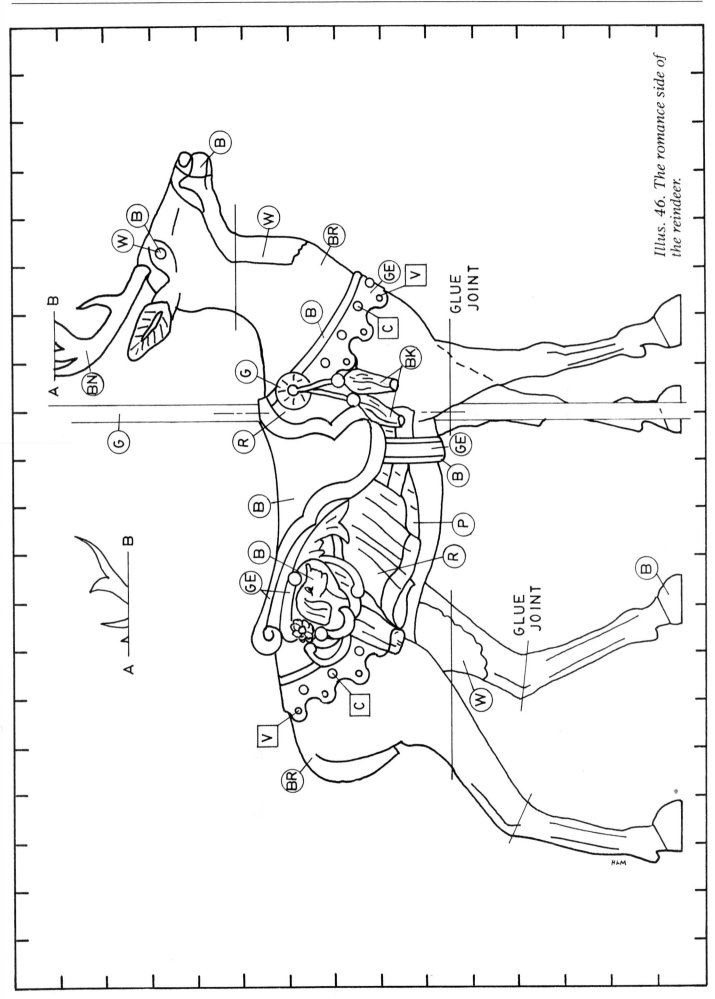

Illus. 46. The romance side of the reindeer.

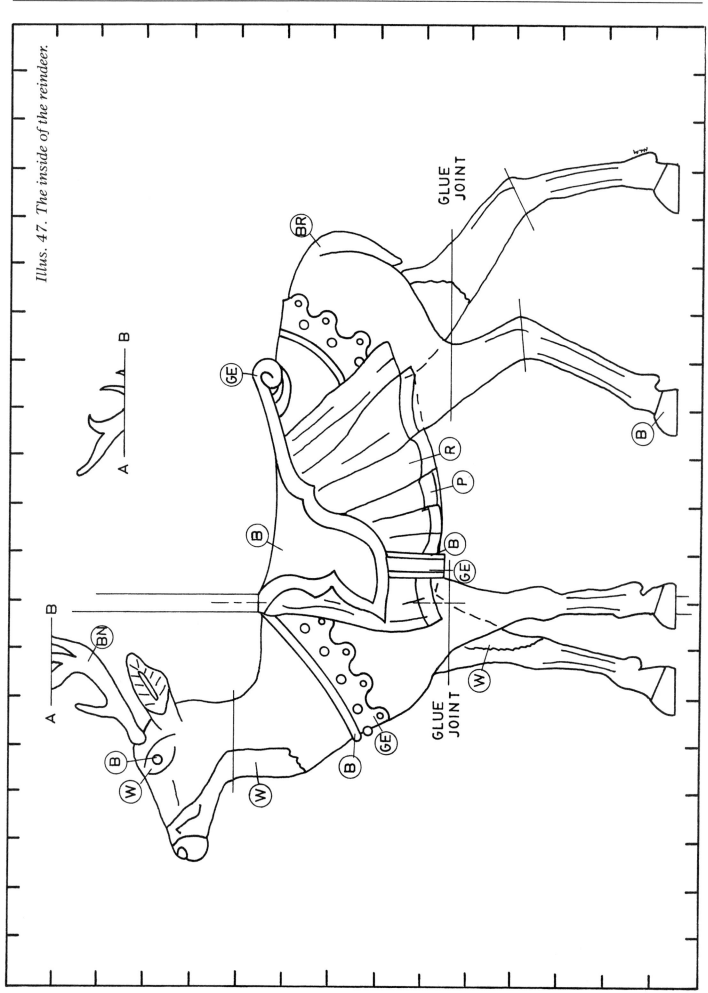

Illus. 47. The inside of the reindeer.

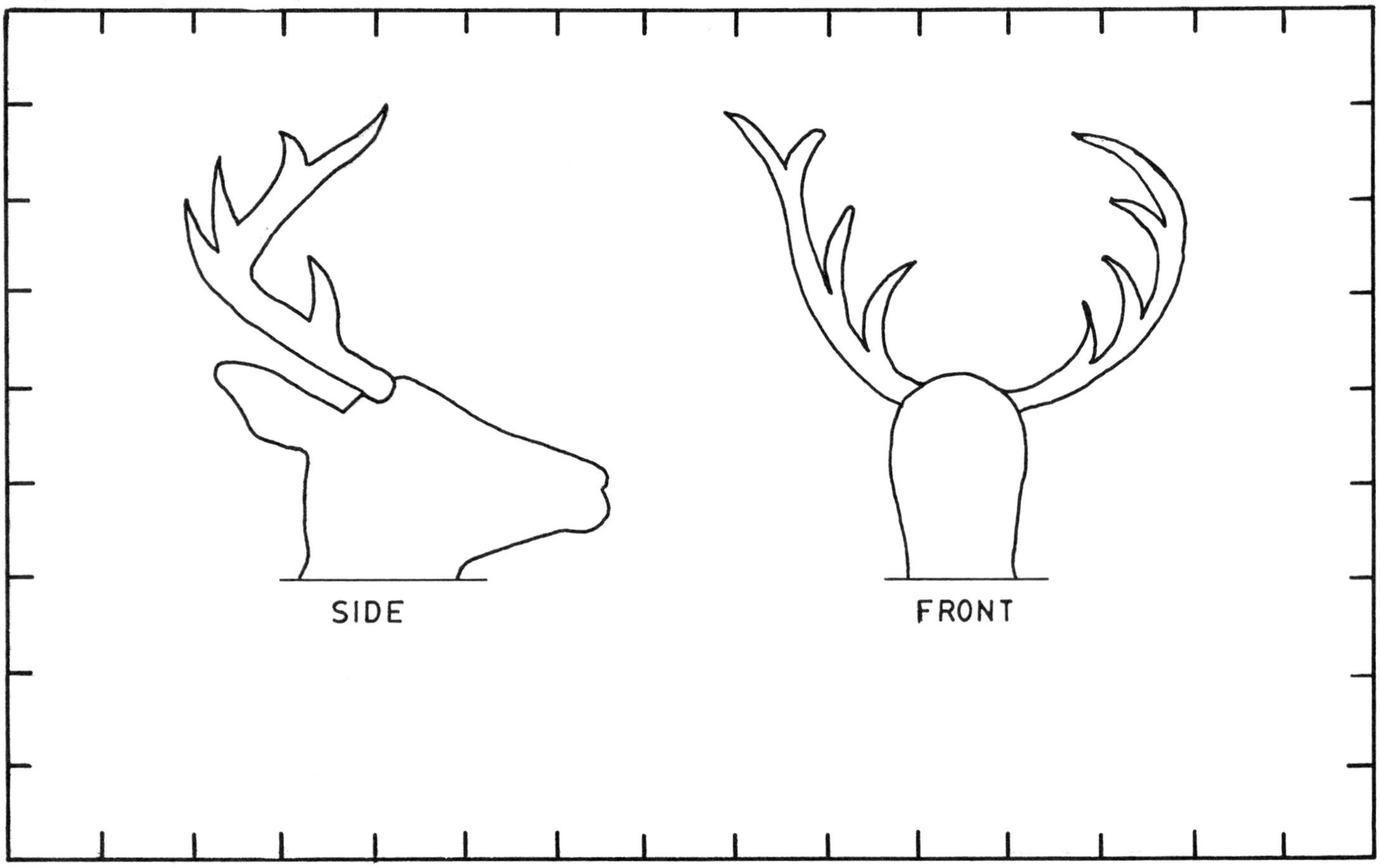

Illus. 48. Reindeer head and rack.

Table 29 Parts List for the Reindeer

Part	*Length*	*Width*	*Thickness*
Head/Rack	2⅜″	2½″	2½″
Body	5¾″	2$\frac{5}{16}$″	1$\frac{5}{16}$″
Right Front Leg	2¾″	$\frac{11}{16}$″	$\frac{5}{16}$″
Left Front Leg	2½″	⅞″	$\frac{5}{16}$″
Right Hind Thigh	1⅝″	$\frac{11}{16}$″	⅝″
Right Hind Leg/Foot	1⅞″	¾″	$\frac{5}{16}$″
Left Hind Thigh	1$\frac{3}{16}$″	$\frac{11}{16}$″	⅝″
Left Hind Leg/Foot	2⅛″	½″	$\frac{5}{16}$″

The complete carving block consists of eight parts, as follow: head/rack, body, right front leg, left front leg, right hind leg (2 sections), and left hind leg (2 sections). Drill a $\frac{3}{16}$″ hole through the body for the pole before gluing the head/rack and legs to the body. Size the end grain of each leg part and glue the head/rack and the legs in place. The head tilts sideways 40° to the right. You can simulate the texture of the body fur by using a ⅛″ high-speed cone-shaped steel cutter in a hand-held motor tool.

Use Illus. 48 as side and front patterns for the head and rack. Jigsaw the side view to shape and then cut out the front view with a knife or hand-held motor tool. Since much of the carving for the rack will involve cross-grain cutting, extra care should be taken in carving this part.

Refer to Illus. 45–47 and Table 30 to carve the final shapes and details. The approximate carving time is 24 hours.

The following table provides the critical dimensions that you will need when carving a ⅛-scale or full-size model:

Table 30   Critical Dimensions for the Reindeer

	⅛ Scale	Full Size
Bottom of foot to top of rack	7⁵⁄₁₆″	58½″
Width of body at pole	1⁵⁄₁₆″	10½″
Width of rear flank	1¼″	10″
Width of saddle at rear	1⁵⁄₁₆″	10½″
Width of head	¾″	6″
Width of nose	⅜″	3″
Distance between eyes	⅝″	5″
Distance between tips of ears	1¹³⁄₁₆″	14½″
Width of rack	2½″	20″
Width of neck at head	⅝″	5″
Width of neck at body	¹⁵⁄₁₆″	7½″
Width of leg at body (front)	⁵⁄₁₆″	2½″
Width of leg at body (hind)	⅝″	5″
Width of leg at knee	⁵⁄₁₆″	2½″
Width of leg (thin area)	³⁄₁₆″	1½″
Width of hoof	⁹⁄₃₂″	2¼″
Length of hoof	½″	4″
Distance between front hooves	¾″	6″
Distance between hind hooves	½″	4″
Width of tail	⅜″	3″

After carving, paint in accordance with the suggested color symbols or use other colors you prefer. Glue six 3-mm crystal rhinestones and six 3-mm violet rhinestones to the breast collar. Glue seven 3-mm crystal rhinestones and seven 3-mm violet rhinestones to the rear flank. Instead of rhinestones, use dots of the appropriate color on the inside.

Insert a 10¼″ length of ³⁄₁₆″ dowel through the hole in the body and glue it in place so that ½″ extends below the bottom of the feet. Make a stand and glue the pole of the completed reindeer to it.

Giraffe

Illus. 49. This giraffe, as might be expected, is the tallest animal on the carousel. It is in the standing position, and, because of its two-tone skin, requires as much time to paint as it does to carve. For a look at the giraffe in full color, turn to page L of the Color Section.

DIRECTIONS

Using Illus. 50 as a plan, cut out the 12 patterns. Attach the tail at line A–B and glue each pattern to wood of the correct thickness as defined in Table 31. The length of each part should follow the direction of the grain.

Table 31 Parts List for the Giraffe

Part	Length	Width	Thickness
Head	2¼″	1⅞″	1″
Neck	2¹⁵⁄₁₆″	1½″	⅞″
Body	5⅛″	2⁵⁄₁₆″	1½″
Right Front Leg	3⅝″	¹³⁄₁₆″	⅝″
Left Front Thigh	1⅝″	¾″	⅝″
Left Front Leg	2″	½″	½″
Right Hind Thigh	1⁹⁄₁₆″	1¼″	¹¹⁄₁₆″
Right Hind Leg	2⅛″	⁹⁄₁₆″	½″
Left Hind Thigh	1⅞″	1⁵⁄₁₆″	¹¹⁄₁₆″
Left Hind Leg	2⅛″	⁹⁄₁₆″	½″
Tail (center)	1″	⅜″	¼″
Tail (end)	2″	½″	⅜″

Make the complete carving block by gluing together 12 parts, as follow: head, neck, body, right front leg, left front leg (2 sections), right hind leg (2 sections), left hind leg (2 sections) and tail (2 sections). Drill a ³⁄₁₆″ hole through the body before gluing the legs and neck in place. Size the end grain of each part and glue the parts to the body. The head should have a 10° sideways tilt to the right. Glue the two bottom sections of the tail together and carve them separately. After you have carved and sanded the giraffe, glue the tail to the body and the right hind leg. Refer to Illus. 49–51 and Table 32 to carve the final shapes and details. The approximate carving time is 19 hours.

The table on page 94 provides the critical dimensions that you will need when carving a ⅛-scale or full-size model.

After carving, paint in accordance with the suggested color symbols. While you are free to use your imagination when selecting colors for other carousel animals, you should stick to the natural skin colors for this carving. Glue a 4-mm crystal rhinestone on the side near the front of the saddle and a 4-mm red rhinestone to the saddle. Glue six 4-mm red rhinestones and five 4-mm crystal rhinestones to the breast collar. Alternate these colors. Glue one 3-mm red rhinestone to the center of the neck bow.

Insert a 10¼″ length of ³⁄₁₆″ dowel through the hole in the body. Glue the dowel so that 4⅛″ extend above the saddle. Glue it in place and add the footrest (Illus. 5) to the pole. Make a stand and glue the pole of the completed giraffe to it.

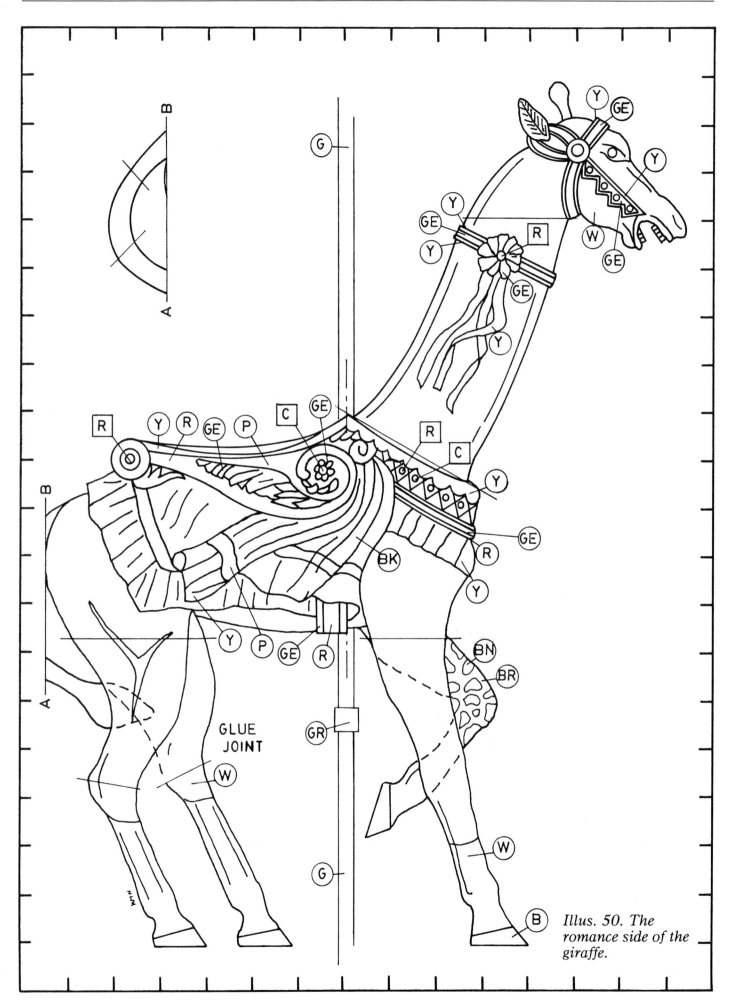

Illus. 50. The romance side of the giraffe.

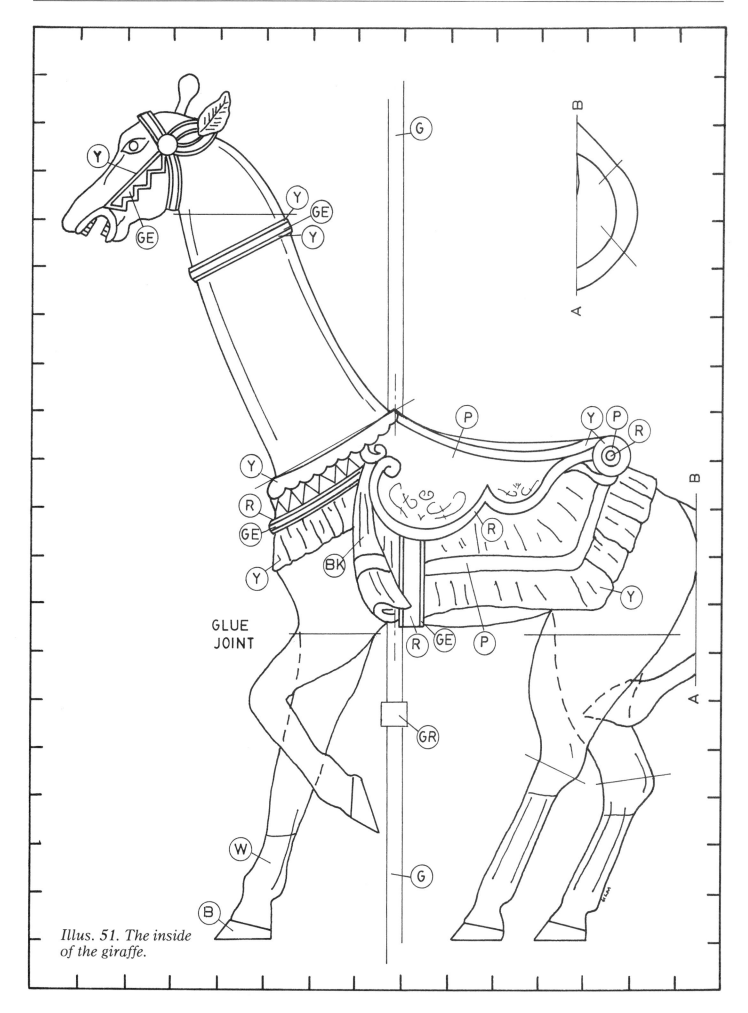

Illus. 51. The inside of the giraffe.

GLUE JOINT

Table 32 Critical Dimensions for the Giraffe

	1/8 Scale	*Full Size*
Bottom of foot to top of horn	8 15/16″	71 1/2″
Width of body at pole	1 1/2″	12″
Width of rear flank	1 3/8″	11″
Width of saddle at rear	1 7/16″	11 1/2″
Width of head	1″	8″
Width of nose	1/2″	4″
Distance between eyes	29/32″	7 1/4″
Distance between tips of ears	1 3/8″	11″
Width of neck at body	7/8″	7″
Width of leg at body (front)	5/8″	5″
Width of leg at body (hind)	11/16″	5 1/2″
Thin area of leg (upper section)	3/8″	3″
Width of leg at knee	1/2″	4″
Thin area of leg (lower section)	1/4″	2″
Width of foot	13/32″	3 1/4″
Length of foot	5/8″	5″
Distance between front feet	1/2″	4″
Distance between hind feet	7/8″	7″
Tail at body	1/4″	2″
Tail at bend	7/32″	1 3/4″

Horse with Feathers

GENERAL NOTES

With his head raised, this prancer, shown in Illus. 52 and 53, is the tallest horse on the Herschell-Spillman carousel. It is also the only one that has feathers as decorations.

DIRECTIONS

Using Illus. 52 as a plan, cut out the nine patterns and glue each pattern to wood of the proper thickness as presented in Table 33. You will have to refer to Illus. 53 for the complete pattern for the left front leg. The length of each part should follow the direction of the grain.

Table 33   Parts List for the Horse with Feathers

Part	Length	Width	Thickness
Head	2⅝″	1½″	⅞″
Body	7″	3⅞″	1½″
Right Front Leg	2⅛″	½″	½″
Left Front Thigh	13/16″	11/16″	½″
Left Front Leg	1¾″	⅝″	½″
Right Hind Thigh	1 9/16″	1⅜″	¾″
Right Hind Leg	2″	⅝″	½″
Left Hind Thigh	2″	1¼″	¾″
Left Hind Leg	2 1/16″	9/16″	½″

The complete carving block is made up of nine parts, as follow: head, body, right front leg, left front leg (2 sections), right hind leg (2 sections) and left hind leg (2 sections). The head is turned approximately 10° to the right. Drill a ³/16″ hole through the body for the pole and a ⅛″ hole for the tail. Size the end grain of each leg part and glue the legs and head to the body. Cut out four horseshoes from ¹/16″ stock and glue one to the bottom of each foot. Refer to Illus. 52 and 53 and Table 34 when carving the final shapes and details. The approximate carving time is 25 hours.

After you have finished the carving and sanding, paint according to the suggested color scheme or in colors that are pleasing to you. Glue one 3-mm blue rhinestone to the headband, fifteen 4-mm amber rhinestones and seven 2-mm blue rhinestones to the breast collar, seven 4-mm red rhinestones to the saddle blanket, and four 3-mm red rhinestones to the top of the rear flank.

Make the tail from approximately 60 strands of heavy-duty dark-brown sewing thread. Each piece should be 3½″ long. Insert a 10¼″ length of ³/16″ dowel through the body and glue it in place so that 4½″

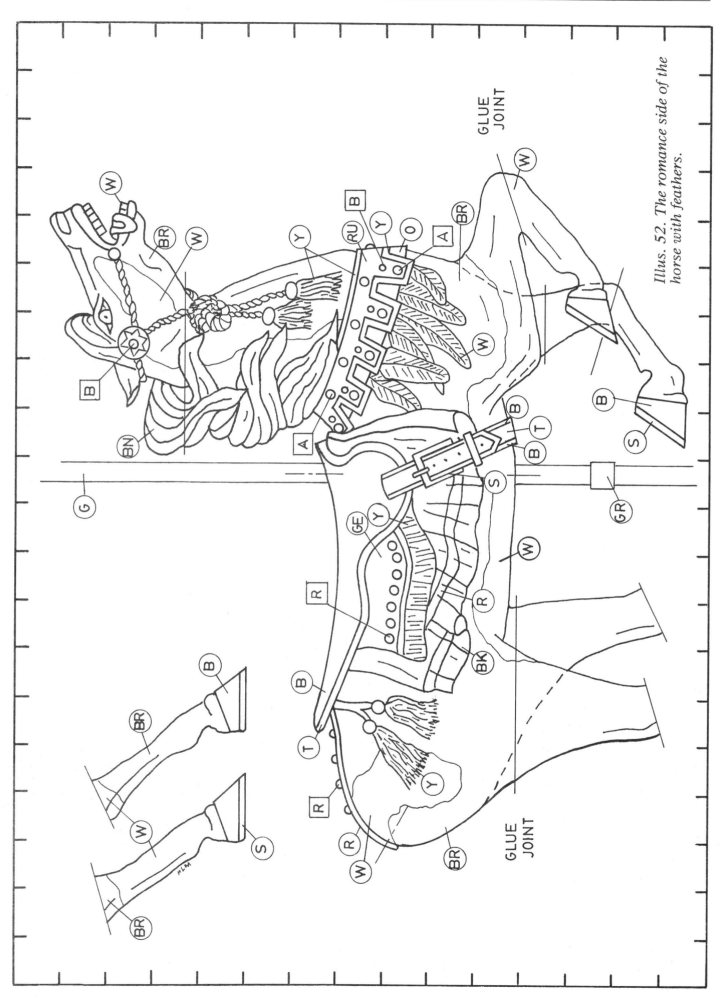

Illus. 52. The romance side of the horse with feathers.

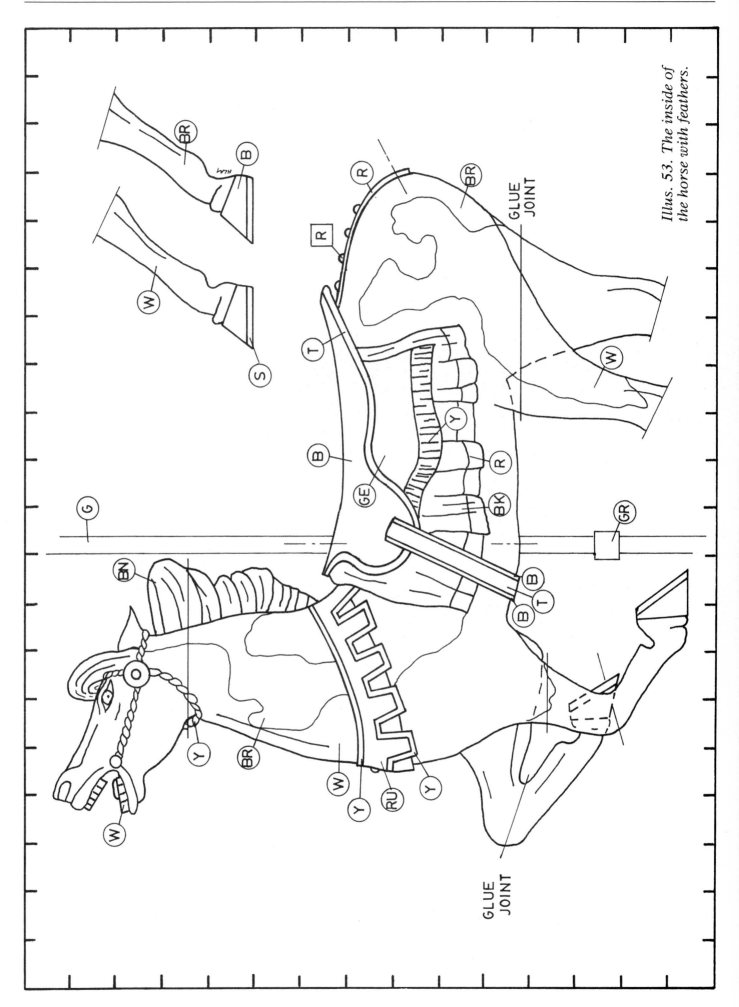

Illus. 53. The inside of the horse with feathers.

extend above the saddle. Glue a footrest (Illus. 5) to the pole. Make a stand and glue the pole of the completed carving to it.

The following table provides the critical dimensions that you will need when carving a ⅛-scale or full-size horse:

Table 34   Critical Dimensions for the Horse with Feathers

	⅛ Scale	Full Size
Bottom of shoe to top of ear	8¼"	66"
Width of head (including mane)	⅞"	7"
Width of nose	½"	4"
Distance between eyes	¾"	6"
Distance between tips of ears	11/16"	5½"
Width of neck at body	15/16"	7½"
Width of neck at head (including rope)	13/16"	6½"
Width of body at pole	1⅜"	11"
Width of rear flank	1½"	12"
Width of saddle at rear	1½"	12"
Width of front leg at body	½"	4"
Width of hind leg at body	¾"	6"
Width of leg at knee	5/16"	2½"
Width of hoof	15/32"	3¾"
Length of hoof	⅝"	5"
Distance between front hooves	¾"	6"
Distance between hind hooves	15/16"	7½"

The Inside Row

The animals on the inside rows are smaller, have fewer decorations, and wear no jewels. In most cases, the romance side and the inside of these animals are very similar or identical. Since these animals are smaller and have fewer trappings than those on the outside rows, they require less time and skill to carve. The procedures outlined on pages 12–20 are still applicable to these animals. The pages that follow in this section present information to help you carve one-eighth reproductions of the smaller and simpler animals located on the inside rows of the carousel.

Ostrich

Illus. 54. One outstanding feature of this strutting bird is its rear tail feathers. The rider sits higher on this creature than on most of the others; as a result, the ostrich is often preferred by the very young rider. For a look at the ostrich in full color, turn to page K of the Color Section.

DIRECTIONS

Using Illus. 55 as a plan, cut out the seven patterns and glue each pattern to wood of the correct thickness as defined in Table 35. The length of each part should follow the direction of the grain.

Table 35   Parts List for the Ostrich

Part	Length	Width	Thickness
Head	1¼″	⅝″	⁹⁄₁₆″
Neck	2¾″	1⅛″	1¼″
Body	4⅝″	2⅜″	1⅝″
Right Leg	2¾″	¹³⁄₁₆″	½″
Right Foot	⅞″	⁷⁄₁₆″	⅝″
Left Leg	2¼″	¾″	½″
Left Foot	¹⁵⁄₁₆″	½″	⅝″

The complete carving block consists of seven parts, as follow: head, neck, body, right leg (2 sections) and left leg (2 sections). Drill a ³⁄₁₆″ hole through the body for the pole before gluing the legs and neck to the body. Size the end grain of each part and glue the head, neck, and legs in place. The head has no sideways tilt.

You can cut the veins of the feathers with a veining tool; however, since much of the cut is made across the grain, there is a real danger that the wood will chip. Therefore, after shaping the feathers with the veining tool, make the veining lines with a woodburning pen rather than with a chisel; the woodburning tool will achieve the same effect with less danger of chipping. Remember, the romance and the inside sides are identical.

Refer to Illus. 54–56 and Table 36 to complete the final shapes and details. The approximate carving time is 16 hours.

The following table provides the critical dimensions that you will need when carving a ⅛-scale or full-size model:

Table 36   Critical Dimensions for the Ostrich

	⅛ Scale	Full Size
Bottom of right foot to top of head	8⁵⁄₁₆″	66½″
Width of body at pole	1⅝″	13″
Width of rear feathers	1⅝″	13″
Width of saddle at rear	1⅛″	9″
Width of head	⁹⁄₁₆″	4½″
Width of beak	⅛″	1″
Distance between eyes	⁹⁄₁₆″	4½″
Width of neck (at body)	1¼″	10″
Width of neck (6″ up from body)	¹³⁄₁₆″	6½″
Width of neck (at thin area)	⁷⁄₁₆″	3½″
Width of leg at body	½″	4″
Width of leg (at thin area)	¼″	2″
Width of foot	⅝″	5″
Length of foot	¾″	6″
Distance between feet	¹⁄₁₆″	½″
Width of tail	1⅝″	13″

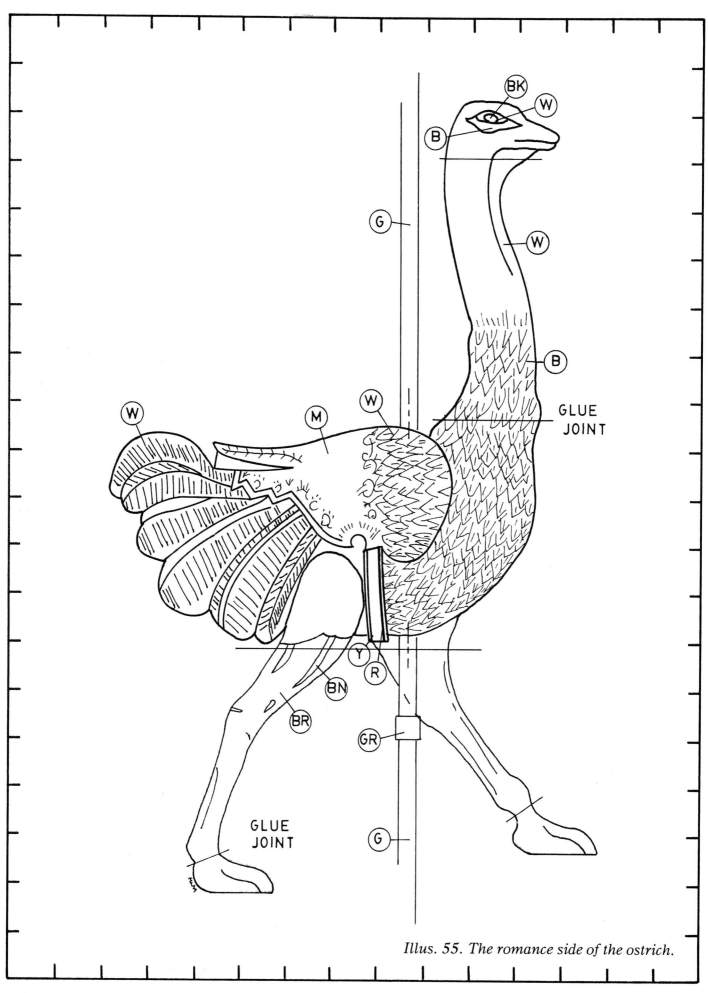

Illus. 55. The romance side of the ostrich.

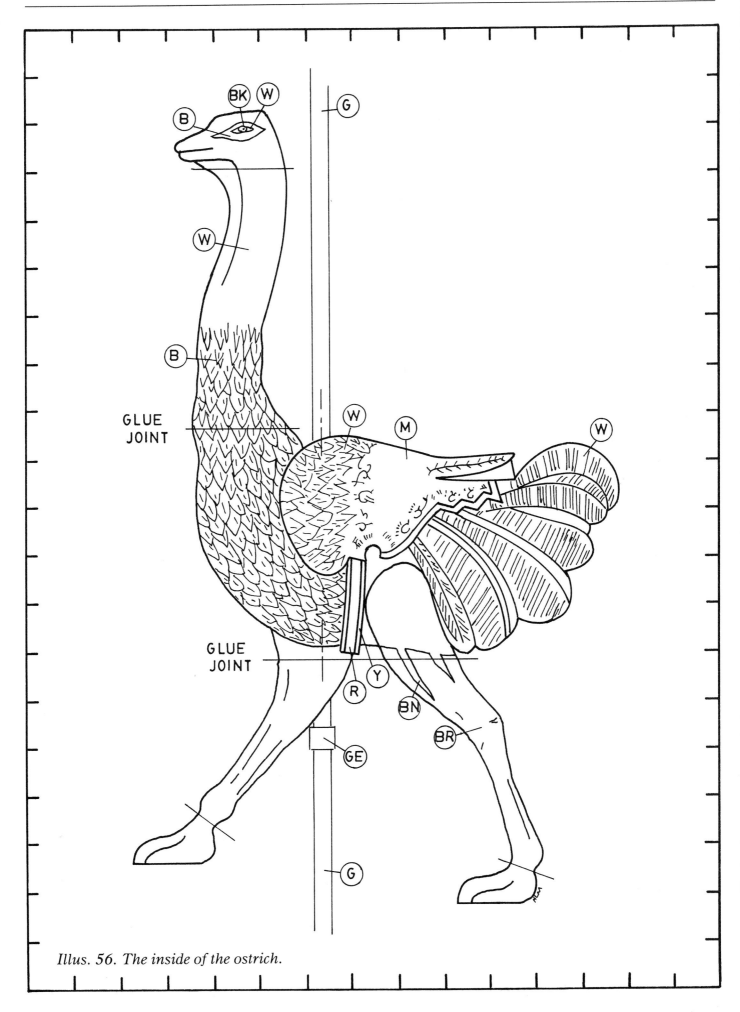

Illus. 56. The inside of the ostrich.

After carving, paint in accordance with the suggested color symbols or according to your own preferences. There are no jewels on this bird. Insert a 10¼″ length of ³⁄₁₆″ dowel through the hole in the body so that 4¾″ extend above the saddle. Glue it in place and add the footrest (Illus. 5) to the pole. Make a stand and insert the pole of the completed ostrich into the hole in the stand.

Jumper with Red Blanket

GENERAL NOTES

This inner-row animal, shown in Illus. 57 and 58, has all four legs in the air and is typical of the numerous horses that are smaller than the more elaborately decorated ones located on the outside row.

DIRECTIONS

Using Illus. 57 as a plan, cut out the ten patterns and glue each pattern to wood of the correct thickness as stated in Table 37. You will have to refer to Illus. 58 for the complete pattern for the left front leg. The length of each part should follow the direction of the grain.

Table 37   Parts List for the Jumper with Red Blanket

Part	Length	Width	Thickness
Body	5½"	3⅞"	1¼"
Right Front Leg	1"	⅜"	½"
Right Front Hoof	¾"	⁷⁄₁₆"	½"
Left Front Leg	1⁹⁄₁₆"	⁷⁄₁₆"	½"
Right Hind Thigh	1⅛"	1⁷⁄₁₆"	⅝"
Right Hind Leg	1⅜"	½"	½"
Right Hind Hoof	¾"	½"	½"
Left Hind Thigh	1⅛"	1⁷⁄₁₆"	⅝"
Left Hind Leg	1⅜"	½"	½"
Left Hind Hoof	¾"	½"	½"

The complete carving block is composed of ten parts, as follow: body, right front leg (2 sections), left front leg, right hind leg (3 sections), and left hind leg (3 sections). The head is not turned and faces straight ahead. The romance side and the inside are identical.

Drill a ³⁄₁₆" hole through the body for the pole and a ⅛" hole for the tail. Size the end grain of each leg part and glue the legs to the body. Cut out four horseshoes from ¹⁄₁₆" stock and glue one to the bottom of each foot. Refer to Illus. 57 and 58 and Table 38 as you carve the final shapes and details. The approximate carving time is 12 hours.

After you have completed the carving and sanding, paint according to the suggested color scheme or in colors that you prefer. There are no jewels on this horse. Make the tail from approximately forty-five 2" lengths of gold sewing thread. Insert a 10¼" length of ³⁄₁₆" dowel through the body and glue it in place so that approximately 4¼" extend above the saddle. Glue a footrest (Illus. 5) to the pole. Make a stand and glue the pole of the finished carving to the stand.

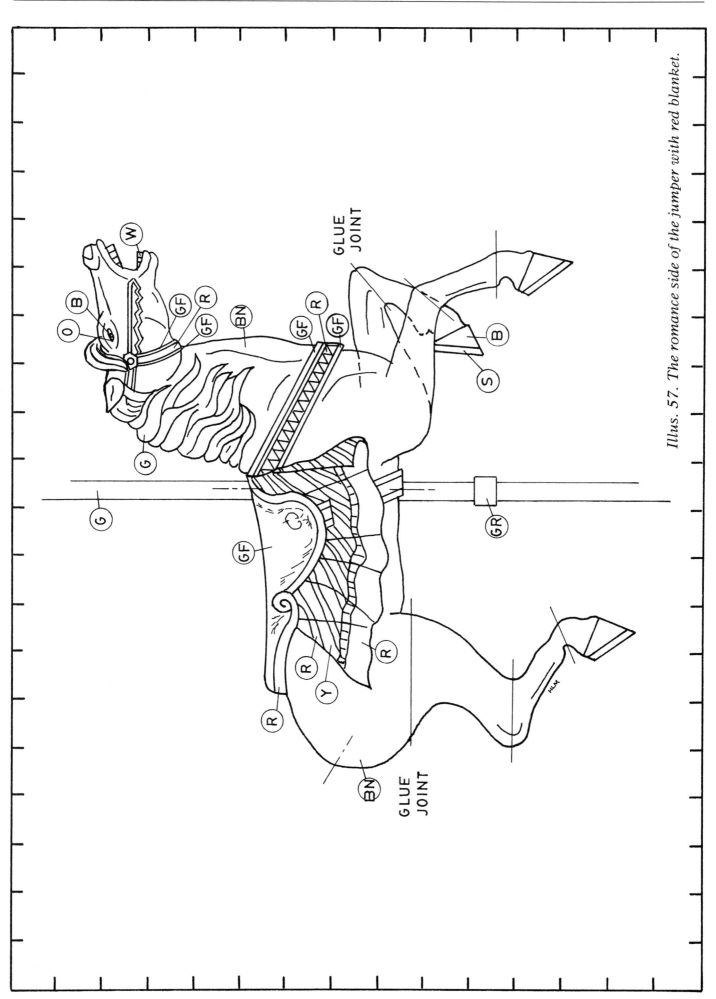

Illus. 57. The romance side of the jumper with red blanket.

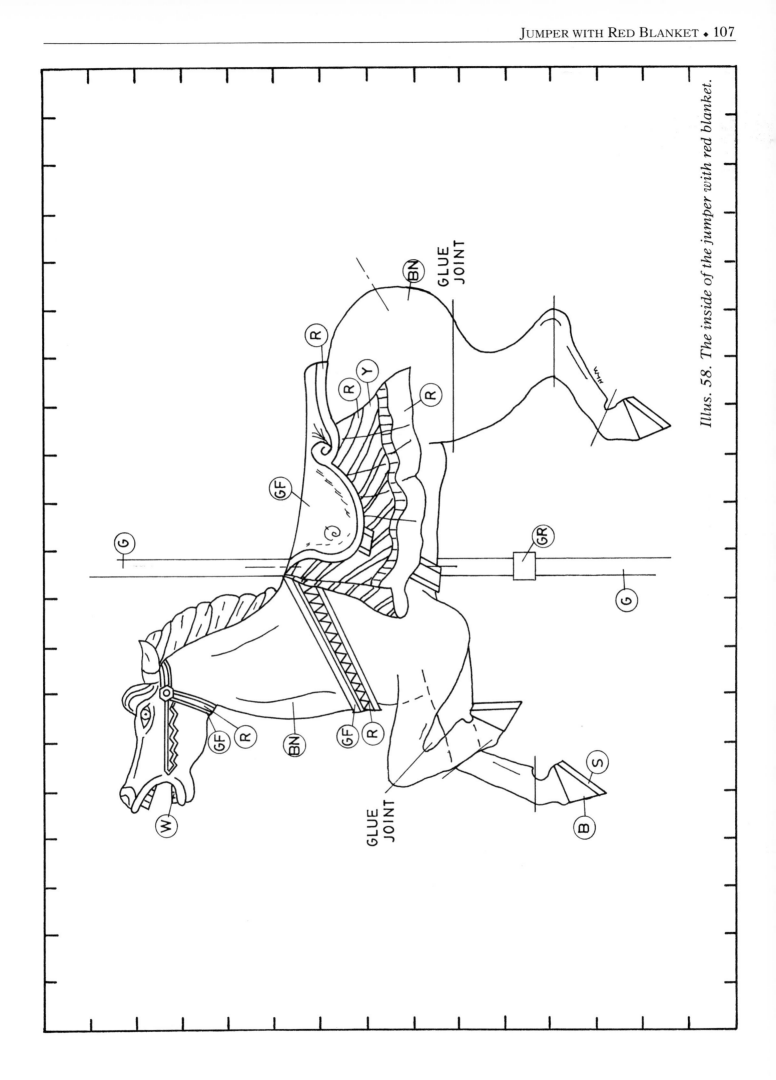

Illus. 58. The inside of the jumper with red blanket.

The following table provides the critical dimensions that you will need when carving a ⅛-scale or full-size model:

Table 38   Critical Dimensions for the Jumper with Red Blanket

	⅛ Scale	Full Size
Distance from rear to chest	4¾"	38"
Width of head (including mane)	¾"	6"
Width of nose	⁷⁄₁₆"	3½"
Distance between eyes	¹¹⁄₁₆"	5½"
Distance between tips of ears	½"	4"
Width of neck at breast band	⅞"	7"
Width of neck at head	½"	4"
Width of body at pole	1⅛"	9"
Width of rear flank	1¼"	10"
Width of saddle at rear	1¼"	10"
Width of front leg at body	⅜"	3"
Width of hind leg at body	⅝"	5"
Width of leg at knee	¼"	2"
Width of hoof	⅜"	3"
Length of hoof	⁹⁄₁₆"	4½"
Distance between front hooves	⁷⁄₁₆"	3½"
Distance between hind hooves	½"	4"

Mule

Illus. 59. The mule is one of a number of domestic animals that have wandered onto the carousel. For a look at the mule in full color, turn to page I of the Color Section.

DIRECTIONS

Using Illus. 60 as a plan, cut out the 11 patterns and glue each pattern to wood of the correct thickness as defined in Table 39. The length of each part should follow the direction of the grain.

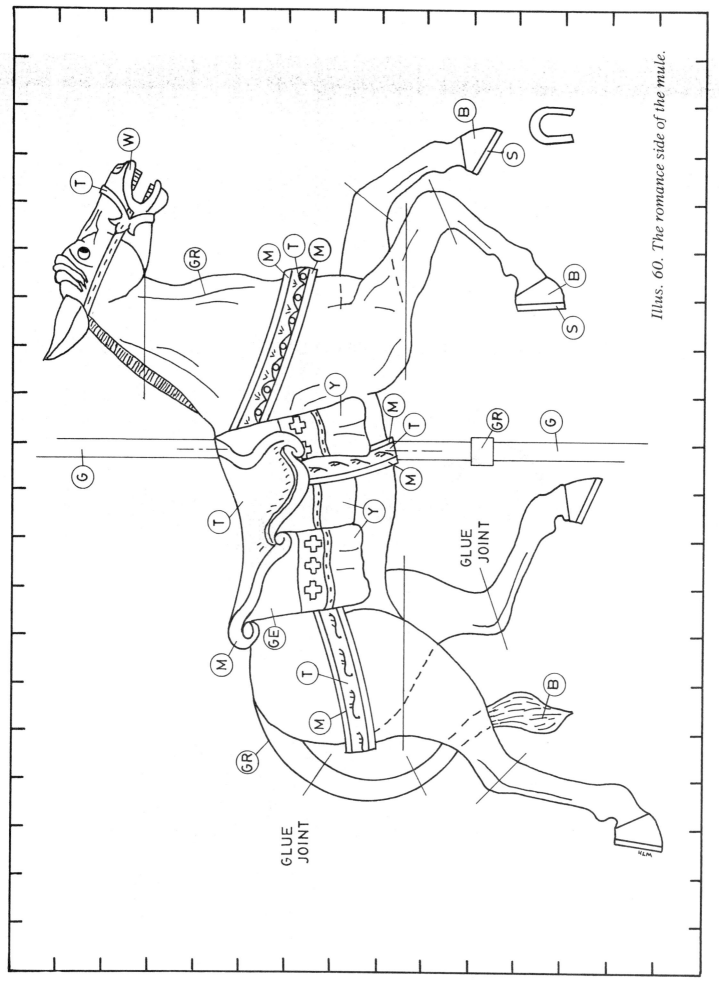

Illus. 60. The romance side of the mule.

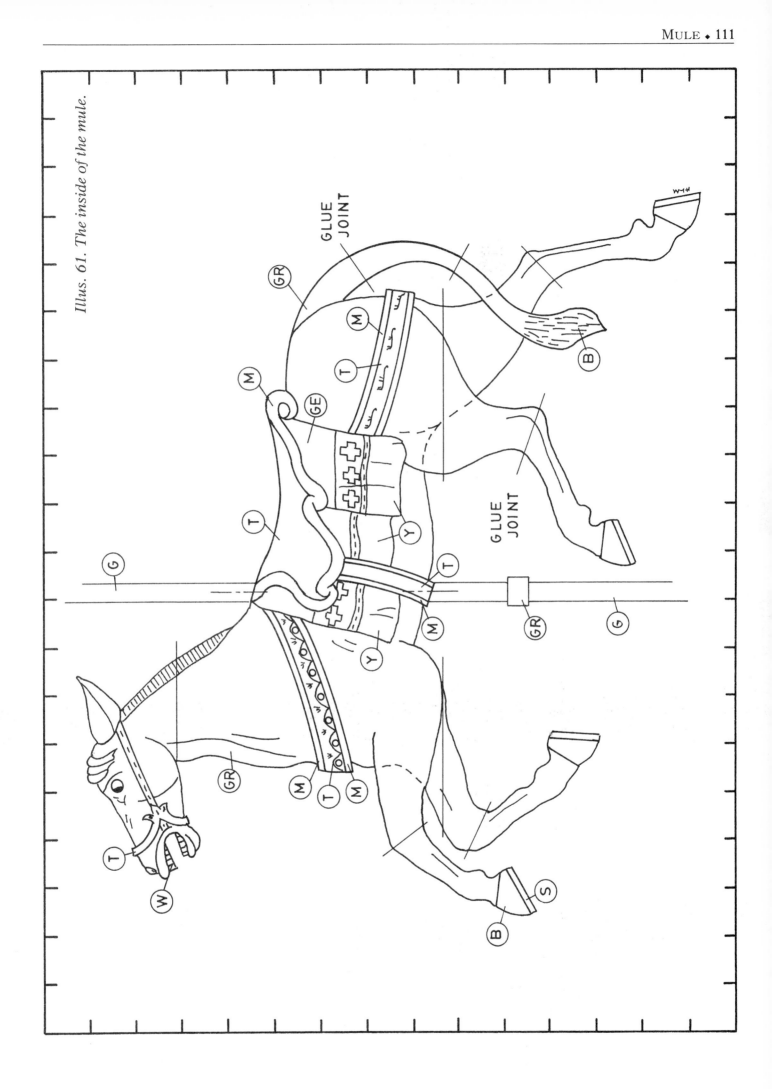

Illus. 61. The inside of the mule.

Table 39   Parts List for the Mule

Part	Length	Width	Thickness
Head	2⁵/₁₆″	1³/₈″	¹³/₁₆″
Body	6³/₁₆″	2¹³/₁₆″	1⁵/₁₆″
Right Front Thigh	1⁷/₈″	½″	³/₈″
Right Front Leg	1¹³/₁₆″	½″	³/₈″
Left Front Leg	1⁵/₈″	½″	³/₈″
Right Hind Thigh	1⁷/₈″	1″	⁵/₈″
Right Hind Leg	2″	⁵/₈″	⁷/₁₆″
Left Hind Thigh	1³/₈″	1¼″	⁵/₈″
Left Hind Leg	1¹⁵/₁₆″	⁹/₁₆″	⁷/₁₆″
Tail (center)	1¼″	⁷/₁₆″	¼″
Tail (end)	1⁷/₈″	⁹/₁₆″	⁷/₁₆″

The complete carving block consists of 11 parts, as follow: head, body, right front leg (2 sections), left front leg, right hind leg (2 sections), left hind leg (2 sections), and tail (2 sections). Drill a ³/₁₆″ hole through the body before gluing the legs in place. Size the end grain of each leg part and glue the legs and head to the body. Glue the bottom two sections of the tail together, carve them separately, and glue them to the body and right leg after you have completely carved and sanded the body.

The head has a sideways tilt of 5° to the right. The romance side and inside are identical. Refer to Illus. 59–61 and Table 40 to complete the final shapes and details. The approximate carving time is 12 hours.

After carving, paint in accordance with the suggested color symbols or in colors you prefer. The square pattern on the saddle blanket can be drawn in paint with a draftsman's ruling pen. There are no jewels on this animal. Insert a 10¼″ length of ³/₁₆″ dowel through the hole in the body with 4⁷/₈″ extended above the saddle. Glue it in place and add the footrest (Illus. 5) to the pole. Make a stand and place the pole of the completed mule on it.

The following table provides the critical dimensions that you will need when carving a ⅛-scale or full-size model:

Table 40   Critical Dimensions for the Mule

	⅛ Scale	Full Size
Distance from tail to breast	5½″	44″
Width of body at pole	1³⁄₁₆″	9½″
Width of rear flank	1³⁄₁₆″	9½″
Width of saddle at rear	1⁵⁄₁₆″	10½″
Width of head	¹³⁄₁₆″	6½″
Width of nose	⅜″	3″
Distance between eyes	½″	4″
Distance between tips of ears	½″	4″
Width of neck at body	¹³⁄₁₆″	6½″
Width of leg at body (front)	⅜″	3″
Width of leg at body (hind)	⅝″	5″
Width of leg at knee	¼″	2″
Width of foot	⅜″	3″
Length of foot	⁹⁄₁₆″	4½″
Distance between front feet	¼″	2″
Distance between hind feet	¼″	2″
Width of tail	¼″	2″

Rooster

Illus. 62. The legs on this rooster are so lifelike that even though they are stationary they appear to be in motion. For a look at the rooster in full color, turn to page D of the Color Section.

DIRECTIONS

Using Illus. 63 as a plan, cut out the five patterns and glue each pattern to wood of the correct thickness as defined in Table 41. The length of each part should follow the direction of the grain.

Table 41 Parts List for the Rooster

Part	Length	Width	Thickness
Body	5⅞″	6⅞″	1½″
Right Leg	1½″	9/16″	½″
Right Foot	¾″	7/16″	⅝″
Left Leg	1 1/16″	½″	½″
Left Foot	⅞″	⅜″	⅝″

The complete carving block consists of five parts, as follow: body, right leg (2 sections), and left leg (2 sections). Drill a 3/16″ hole through the body before gluing the right leg in place. Size the end grain of the legs and feet and glue them in place. The head is facing forward with no sideways tilt. The romance side and the inside are identical, with the exception of a slightly different feather pattern. Refer to Illus. 62–64 and Table 42 to complete the final shapes and details. The approximate carving time is 18 hours.

The following table provides the critical dimensions that you will need when carving a ⅛-scale or full-size model:

Table 42 Critical Dimensions for the Rooster

	⅛ Scale	Full Size
Bottom of foot to top of comb	7¾″	62″
Width of body at pole	1½″	12″
Width of saddle at rear	1½″	12″
Width of body at front breast	⅞″	7″
Width of head (back of comb)	⅝″	5″
Distance between eyes	13/16″	6½″
Width of comb on head	5/16″	2½″
Width of neck at body	⅞″	7″
Width of leg at body	½″	4″
Width of foot	9/16″	4½″
Width of leg at foot	¼″	2″
Length of foot	⅞″	7″
Distance between feet	¾″	6″
Width of tail (top) at saddle	7/16″	3½″
Width of tail at bottom	⅝″	5″
Width of tail at rear	⅛″	1″

After carving, paint in accordance with the suggested color symbols or paint in colors that suit you. There are no jewels on this bird. Insert a 10¼″ length of 3/16″ dowel through the hole in the body and have it extend 4″ above the saddle. Glue it in place and add the footrest (Illus. 5) to the pole. Make a stand and place the pole of the completed rooster in the hole in it.

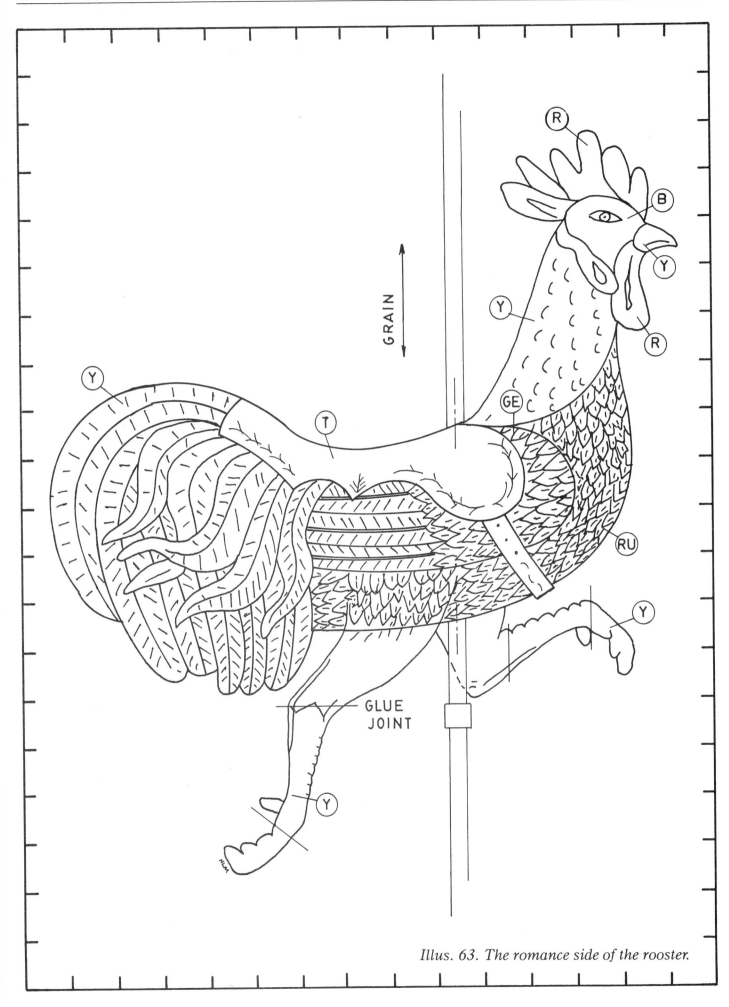

GRAIN

GLUE JOINT

Illus. 63. The romance side of the rooster.

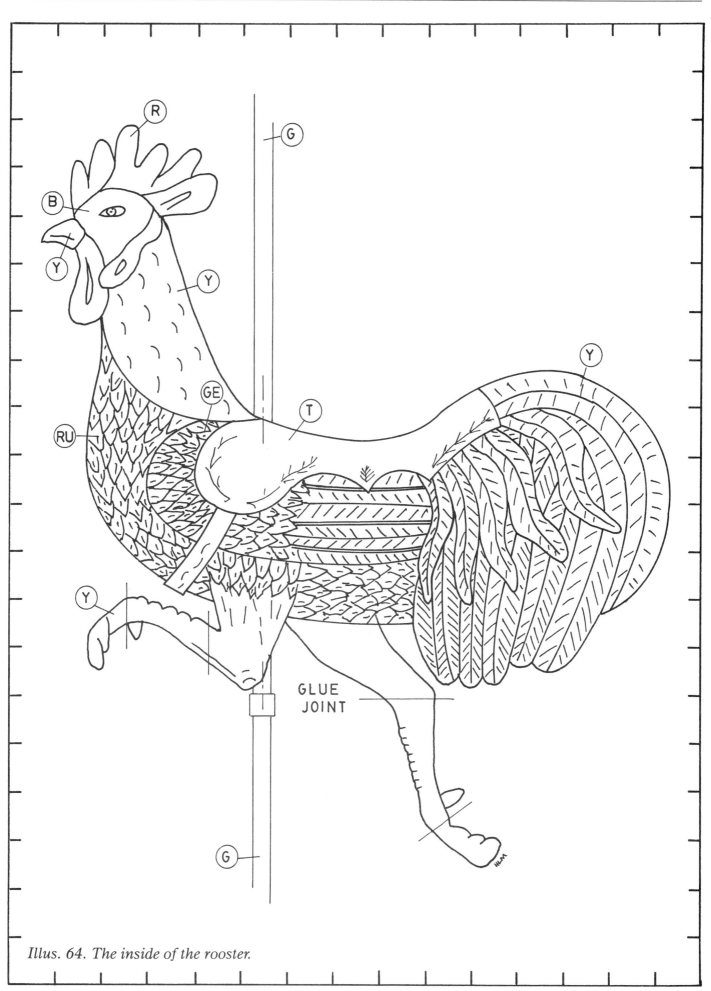

Illus. 64. The inside of the rooster.

Indian's Horse

Illus. 65. This horse is typical of many carousel horses that reflect aspects of the American past. The Indian, quiver, and rope attract many adventurous youngsters. For a look at the Indian's horse in full color, turn to page N of the Color Section.

DIRECTIONS

Using Illus. 66 as a plan, cut out the ten patterns and glue each pattern to wood of the correct thickness as listed in Table 43. The length of each part should follow the direction of the grain.

Table 43   Parts List for the Indian's Horse

Part	Length	Width	Thickness
Head	1⅞″	⅞″	⅝″
Body	5¾″	2⅞″	1¼″
Right Front Leg	1⁵⁄₁₆″	⅜″	⅜″
Right Front Hoof	⁹⁄₁₆″	⁷⁄₁₆″	⁷⁄₁₆″
Left Front Thigh	¾″	⅝″	⅜″
Left Front Leg	1⁹⁄₁₆″	½″	⁷⁄₁₆″
Right Hind Thigh	1½″	¹⁵⁄₁₆″	⅝″
Right Hind Leg	1⅝″	⅞″	⁷⁄₁₆″
Left Hind Thigh	1″	1⅜″	⅝″
Left Hind Leg	1¹³⁄₁₆″	⁹⁄₁₆″	⁷⁄₁₆″

The complete carving block consists of ten parts, as follow: head, body, right front leg (2 sections), left front leg (2 sections), right hind leg (2 sections), and left hind leg (2 sections). Drill a ³⁄₁₆″ hole through the body for the pole and a ⅛″ hole for the tail before attaching the legs. Size the end grain of the legs and glue them to the body. The head has a 5° sideways tilt to the right.

Carve the rope and feathers on the arrows with a knife; add the final details with a woodburning pen. Refer to Illus. 65–67 and Table 44 to complete the final shapes and details. The approximate carving time is 14 hours.

The following table provides the critical dimensions that you will need when carving a ⅛-scale or full-size model:

Table 44   Critical Dimensions for the Indian's Horse

	⅛ Scale	Full Size
Bottom of left hind foot to top of head	6¼″	50″
Width of body at pole	1¼″	10″
Width of rear flank	1¼″	10″
Width of saddle at rear	1¼″	10″
Width of head	¹⁹⁄₃₂″	4¾″
Width of nose	¹³⁄₃₂″	3¼″
Distance between eyes	⅝″	5″
Distance between tips of ears	½″	4″
Width of neck at body	¹³⁄₁₆″	6½″
Width of neck at head	½″	4″
Width of leg at body (front)	⅜″	3″
Width of leg at body (hind)	⅝″	5″
Width of leg at knee	¼″	2″
Width of foot	¹³⁄₃₂″	3¼″
Length of foot	⁹⁄₁₆″	4½″
Distance between front feet	½″	4″
Distance between hind feet	⅝″	5″

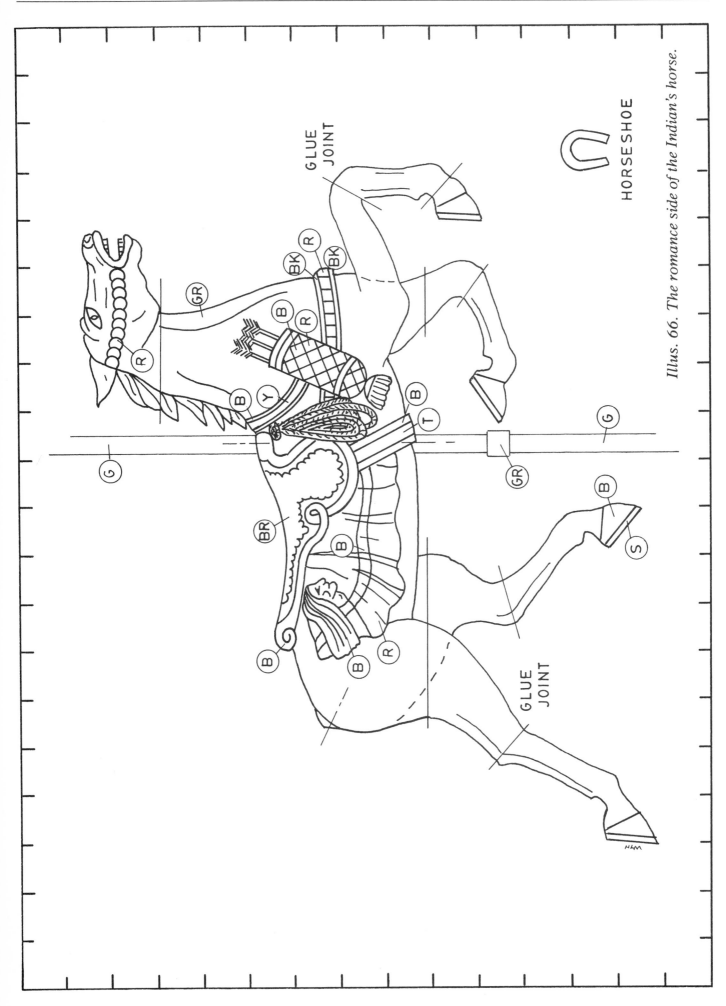

Illus. 66. The romance side of the Indian's horse.

HORSESHOE

GLUE JOINT

GLUE JOINT

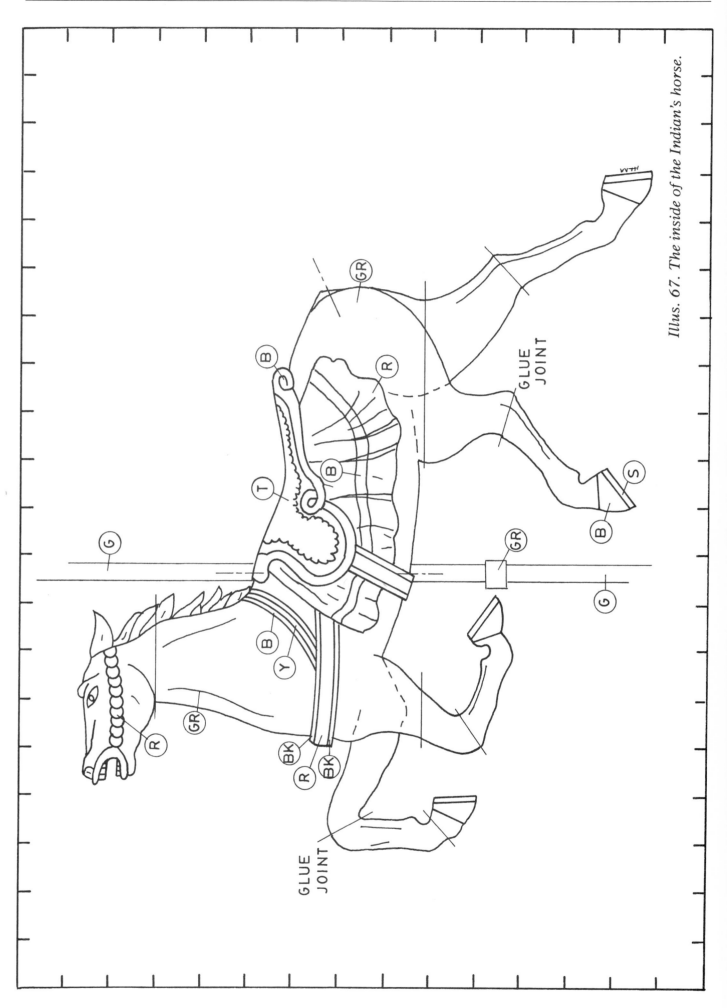

Illus. 67. The inside of the Indian's horse.

After carving, paint as suggested by the color symbols or in colors that are pleasing to you. There are no jewels on this horse. Make the tail from forty-five 2″ long pieces of heavy-duty black sewing thread. Insert a 10¼″ length of ³⁄₁₆″ dowel through the hole in the body with 4½″ above the saddle. Glue it in place and add the footrest (Illus. 5) to the pole. Make a stand and mount the completed horse in it.

Horse with Plaid Blanket

GENERAL NOTES

This jumper, shown in Illus. 68 and 69, is representative of many horses on the smaller carousels or on the inside rows of the larger rides.

DIRECTIONS

Using Illus. 68 as a plan, cut out the 12 patterns and glue them to wood of the proper thickness as listed in Table 45. Refer to Illus. 69 for the complete pattern for the left front leg. The length of each part should follow the direction of the grain.

Table 45   Parts List for the Horse with Plaid Blanket

Part	Length	Width	Thickness
Head	2⅜″	1³⁄₁₆″	¾″
Body	5½″	3⅛″	1¼″
Right Front Leg	1⅛″	⅜″	⅜″
Right Front Hoof	⅝″	⁷⁄₁₆″	⅜″
Left Front Leg	1¼″	⁷⁄₁₆″	⅜″
Left Front Hoof	⁹⁄₁₆″	⁷⁄₁₆″	⅜″
Right Hind Thigh	1³⁄₁₆″	1⅜″	⅝″
Right Hind Leg	1½″	½″	⅜″
Right Hind Hoof	¹¹⁄₁₆″	½″	⅜″
Left Hind Thigh	1³⁄₁₆″	1⅜″	⅝″
Left Hind Leg	1½″	½″	⅜″
Left Hind Hoof	¹¹⁄₁₆″	½″	⅜″

The complete carving block is composed of 12 parts, as follow: head, body, right front leg (2 sections), left front leg (2 sections), right hind leg (3 sections), and left hind leg (3 sections). The head is turned approximately 5° to the right.

Drill a ³⁄₁₆″ hole through the body for the pole and a ⅛″ hole for a tail. Size the end grain of each leg part and glue the legs and head to the body. Cut out four horseshoes from ¹⁄₁₆″ thick stock and glue one to the bottom of each foot. Illus. 68 and 69 and Table 46 will serve to help you carve the final shapes and details. The romance side and the inside are identical. The approximate carving time is 12 hours.

Table 46, on page 126, provides the critical dimensions that you will need when carving a ⅛-scale or full-size horse.

After carving, paint according to the suggested color scheme or in colors that are pleasing to you. There are no jewels on this horse. Make the tail from approximately forty-five 2½″ long strands of gold sewing thread. Insert a 10¼″ length of ³⁄₁₆″ dowel through the body and glue it in place so that approximately 4″ extend above the

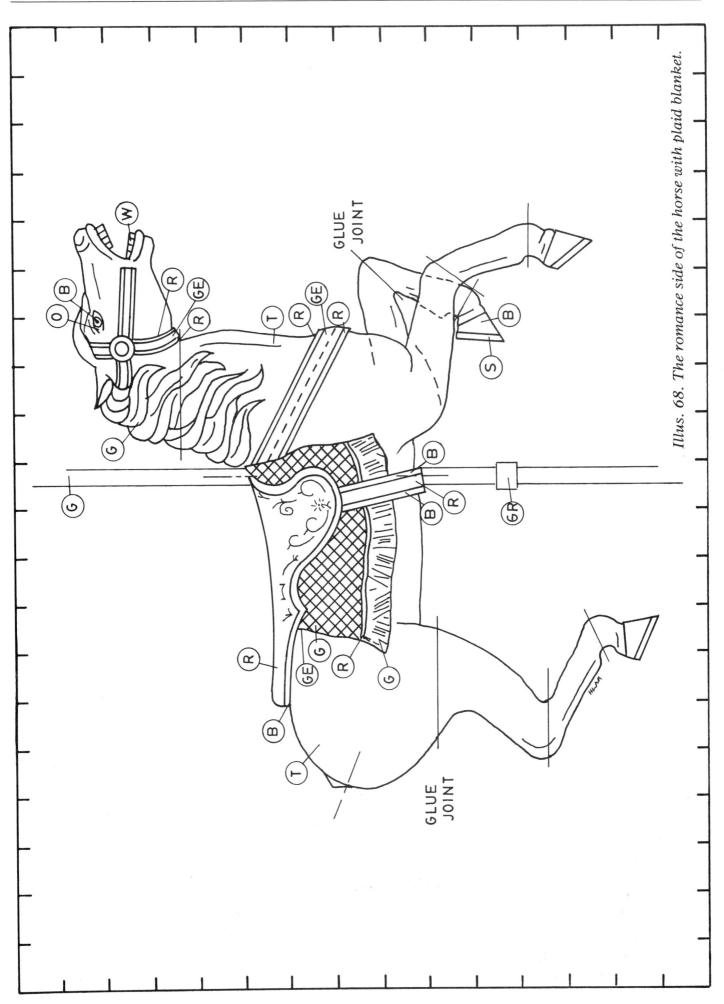

Illus. 68. The romance side of the horse with plaid blanket.

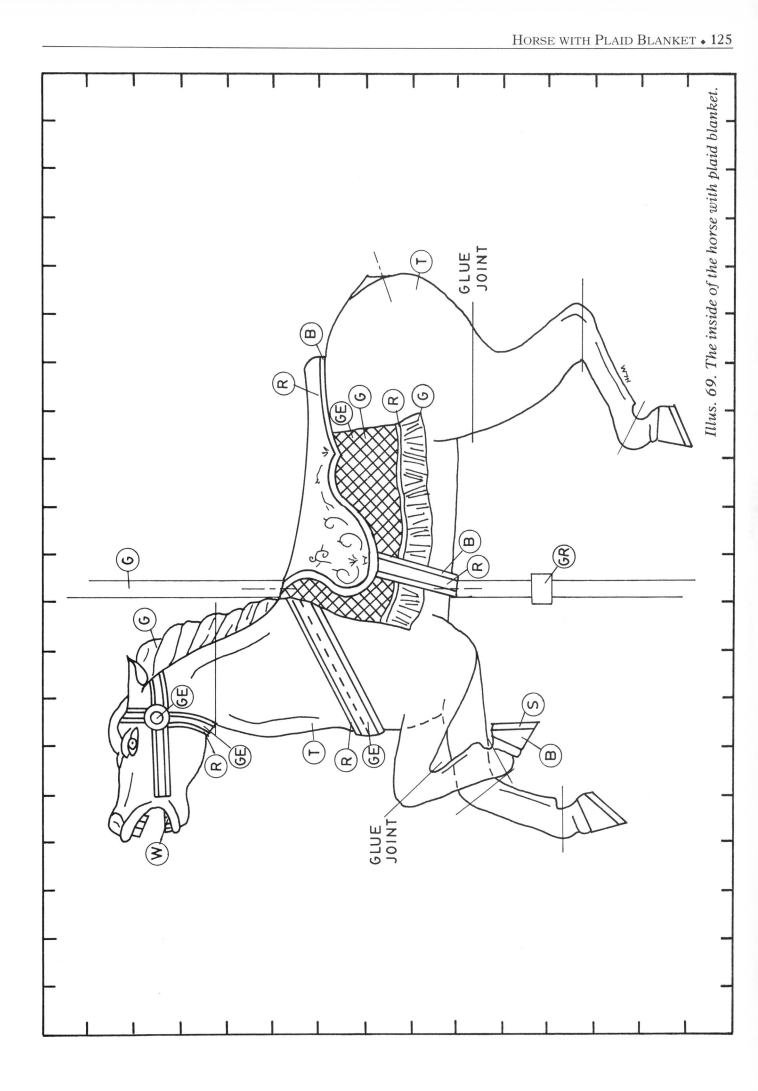

Illus. 69. The inside of the horse with plaid blanket.

saddle. Glue a footrest (Illus. 5) to the pole. Make a stand and glue the pole of the completed carving to it.

Table 46   Critical Dimensions for the Horse with Plaid Blanket

	⅛ Scale	Full Size
Distance from rear to chest	4¾″	38″
Width of head (including mane)	¾″	6″
Width of nose	⅜″	3″
Distance between eyes	⅝″	5″
Distance between tips of ears	¾″	6″
Width of neck at breast band	⅞″	7″
Width of neck at head	½″	4″
Width of body at pole	1¼″	10″
Width of rear flank	1¼″	10″
Width of saddle at rear	1¼″	10″
Width of front leg at body	⅜″	3″
Width of hind leg at body	⅝″	5″
Width of leg at knee	¼″	2″
Width of hoof	⅜″	3″
Length of hoof	½″	4″
Distance between front hooves	⁷⁄₁₆″	3½″
Distance between hind hooves	½″	4″

Horse with Orange Streamers

GENERAL NOTES

This free-spirited animal, shown in Illus. 70 and 71, presents another challenge to carvers. The orange streamers draw your eyes to this steed.

DIRECTIONS

Using Illus. 70 as a plan, cut out the ten patterns and glue them to wood of the correct thickness as listed in Table 47. The length of each part should follow the direction of the grain.

Table 47   Parts List for the Horse with Orange Streamers

Part	Length	Width	Thickness
Head	1¹³⁄₁₆″	1³⁄₁₆″	¾″
Body	5³⁄₈″	2⅝″	1¼″
Right Front Leg	1″	⁷⁄₁₆″	⅜″
Right Front Hoof	¾″	⁷⁄₁₆″	⅜″
Left Front Leg	1″	⅜″	⅜″
Left Front Hoof	⅝″	⁵⁄₁₆″	⅜″
Right Hind Thigh	2″	½″	⅝″
Right Hind Leg	1⅞″	⁹⁄₁₆″	⅜″
Left Hind Thigh	1¼″	¾″	⅝″
Left Hind Leg	1¹³⁄₁₆″	½″	⅜″

The complete carving block consists of ten parts, as follow: head, body, right front leg (2 sections), left front leg (2 sections), right hind leg (2 sections), and left hind leg (2 sections). The head is turned 5° to the right.

Drill a ³⁄₁₆″ hole through the body for the pole and a ⅛″ hole for the tail. Size the end grain of each leg part and glue the head and legs to the body. Cut out four horseshoes from ¹⁄₁₆″ stock and glue one to the bottom of each foot. Refer to Illus. 70 and 71 and Table 48 when carving the final shapes and details. The inside is the same as the romance side except it contains only the blanket—the orange streamers are missing. The approximate carving time is 12 hours.

Table 48, on page 130, provides the critical dimensions that you will need when carving a ⅛-scale or full-size horse.

After carving, paint as suggested or select your own color scheme. There are no jewels on this horse. Make the tail from approximately forty-five 2″ lengths of black sewing thread. Glue the tail into the ⅛″ hole. Insert a 10¼″ length of ³⁄₁₆″ dowel through the body and

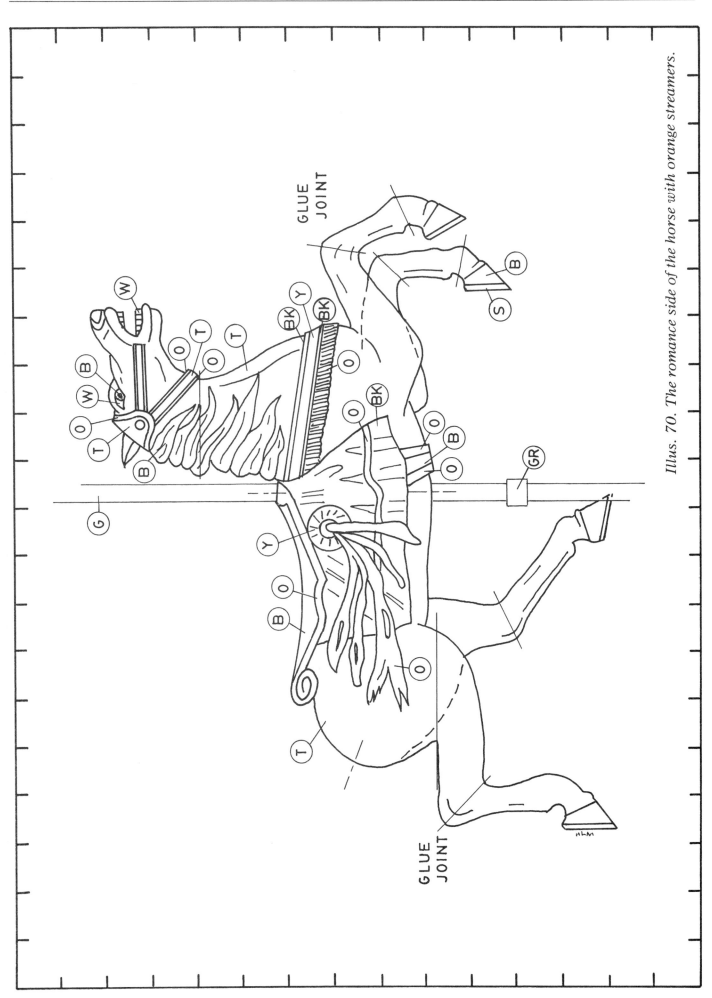

Illus. 70. The romance side of the horse with orange streamers.

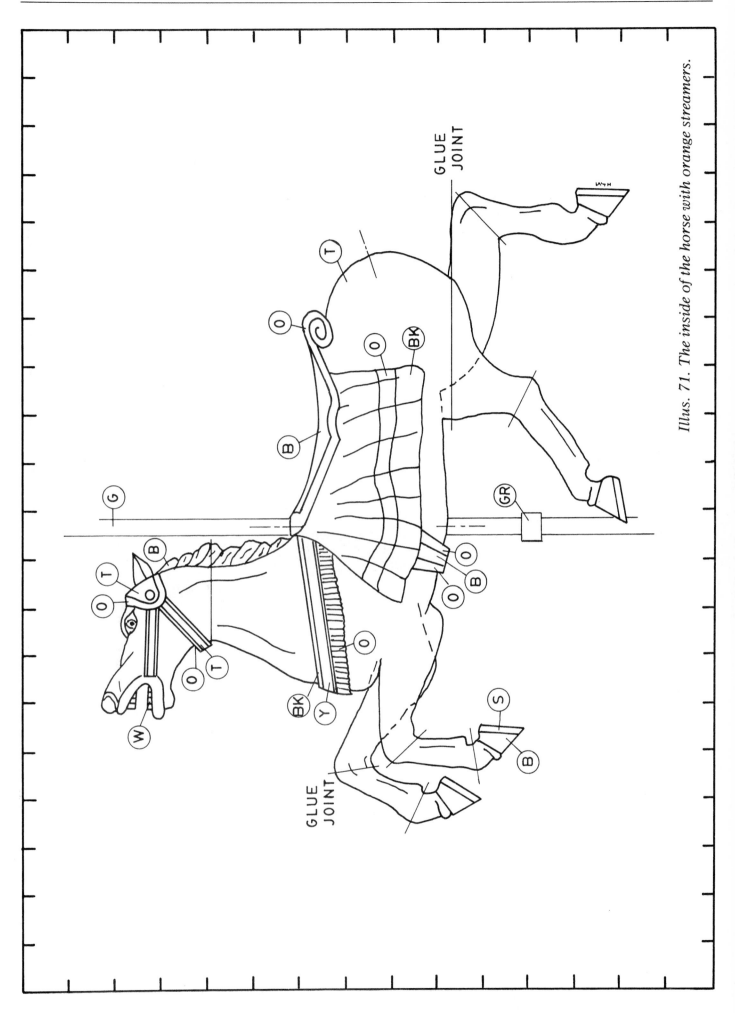

Illus. 71. The inside of the horse with orange streamers.

glue it in place so that approximately 4½″ extend above the saddle. Glue a footrest (Illus. 5) to the pole. Make a stand and glue the pole of the completed horse to it.

Table 48   Critical Dimensions for the Horse
with Orange Streamers

	⅛ Scale	Full Size
Distance from rear leg to front right hoof	6¾″	54″
Width of head (including mane)	¾″	6″
Width of nose	⅜″	3″
Distance between eyes	⅝″	5″
Distance between tips of ears	½″	4″
Width of neck at chest	1¼″	10″
Width of neck at head	⅝″	5″
Width of body at pole	1⅛″	9″
Width of rear flank	1¼″	10″
Width of saddle at rear	1¼″	10″
Width of front leg at body	⅜″	3″
Width of hind leg at body	⅝″	5″
Width of leg at knee	¼″	2″
Width of hoof	⅜″	3″
Length of hoof	9⁄16″	4½″
Distance between front hooves	⅝″	5″
Distance between hind hooves	¾″	6″

American Jumper

Illus. 72. The patriotic theme, so often a part of the carousel, is exemplified in this jumper, which proudly displays the American flag. For a look at this horse in full color, turn to page H of the Color Section.

DIRECTIONS

Using Illus. 73 as a plan, cut out the eight patterns and glue each pattern to wood of the correct thickness as listed in Table 49. The length of each part should follow the direction of the grain.

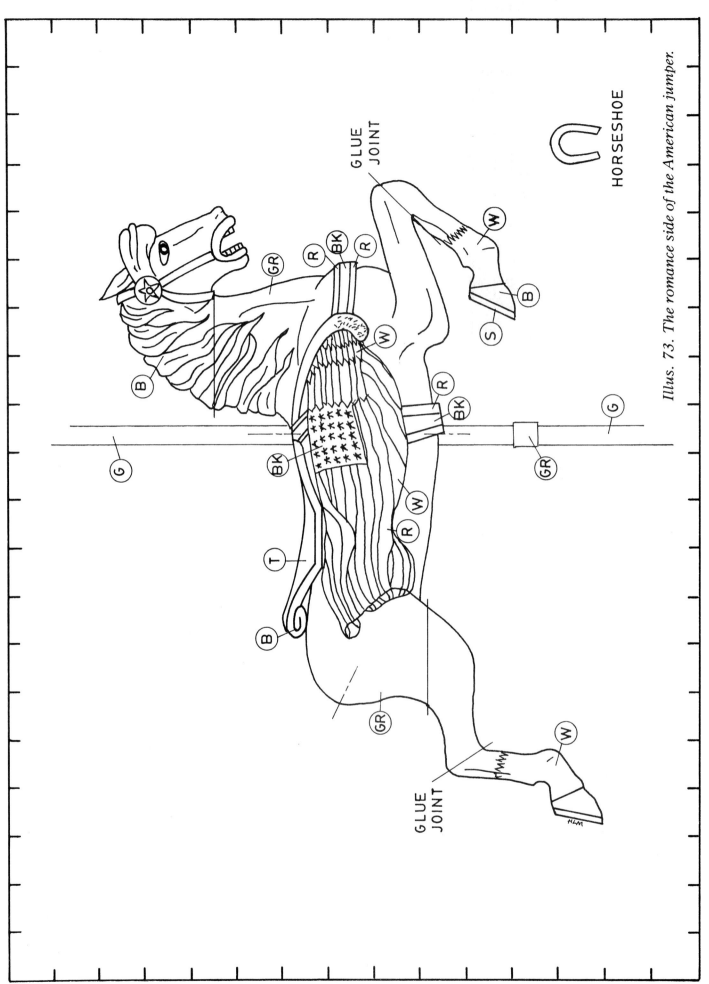

Illus. 73. The romance side of the American jumper.

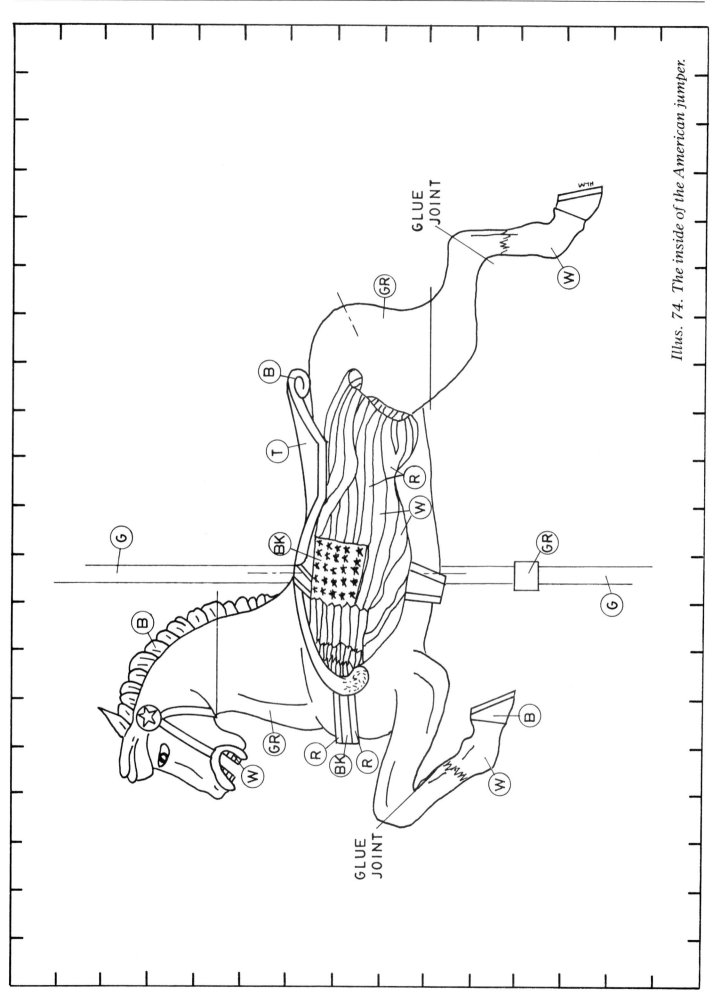

Illus. 74. The inside of the American jumper.

Table 49   Parts List for the American Jumper

Part	Length	Width	Thickness
Head	2⅛″	1¹¹⁄₁₆″	¹³⁄₁₆″
Body	5⁷⁄₁₆″	2⁹⁄₁₆″	1¼″
Right Front Leg	2″	⅝″	⁷⁄₁₆″
Left Front Leg	2″	⅝″	⁷⁄₁₆″
Right Hind Thigh	1¾″	⅝″	⁹⁄₁₆″
Right Hind Leg	1¾″	⅝″	⁷⁄₁₆″
Left Hind Thigh	1¾″	⅝″	⁹⁄₁₆″
Left Hind Leg	1¾″	⅝″	⁷⁄₁₆″

The complete carving block consists of eight parts, as follow: head, body, right front leg, left front leg, right hind leg (2 sections) and left hind leg (2 sections). Drill a ³⁄₁₆″ hole through the body for the pole and a ⅛″ hole for the tail before gluing the legs to the body. Size the end grain of the legs and glue them in place. Cut out four horse-shoes from ¹⁄₁₆″ thick stock and glue one to each hoof.

The head has a 5° sideways tilt to the right. The romance side and the inside are identical. The front and hind legs should be in alignment. Refer to Illus. 72–74 and Table 50 to complete the final shapes and details. The approximate carving time is 13 hours.

The following table provides the critical dimensions that you will need when carving a ⅛-scale or full-size model:

Table 50   Critical Dimensions for the American Jumper

	⅛ Scale	Full Size
Distance from rump to breast	4⅝″	37″
Width of body at pole	1³⁄₁₆″	9½″
Width of rear flank	1³⁄₁₆″	9½″
Width of saddle at rear	1¼″	10″
Width of front of chest	1¼″	10″
Width of head	¹³⁄₁₆″	6½″
Width of nose	⁷⁄₁₆″	3½″
Distance between eyes	¹¹⁄₁₆″	5½″
Distance between tips of ears	⁹⁄₁₆″	4½″
Width of leg at body (front)	⁷⁄₁₆″	3½″
Width of leg at body (hind)	⁹⁄₁₆″	4½″
Width of leg at knee	⅜″	3″
Width of hoof	¹³⁄₃₂″	3¼″
Length of hoof	⁹⁄₁₆″	4½″
Distance between front hooves	½″	4″
Distance between hind hooves	½″	4″

After carving, paint according to the suggested color symbols or in colors that are pleasing to you. There are no jewels on this horse. Make the tail from forty-five 2″ long pieces of heavy-duty black sewing thread. Insert a 10¼″ length of ³⁄₁₆″ dowel through the hole in the body with 4½″ below the belly, and glue it in place. Add the footrest (Illus. 5) to the pole. Make a stand and place the pole of the completed horse in it.

Pig

Illus. 75. This pig, caught in the act of stealing corn, has carried the evidence onto the carousel. For a look at the pig in full color, turn to page D of the Color Section.

DIRECTIONS

Using Illus. 76 as a plan, cut out the seven patterns and glue each pattern to wood of the correct thickness as listed in Table 51. The length of each part should follow the direction of the grain.

The complete carving block consists of seven parts, as follows: body, right front leg, left front leg, right hind leg (2 sections) and left hind leg (2 sections). Drill a ³⁄₁₆″ hole through the body for the pole

Table 51   Parts List for the Pig

Part	Length	Width	Thickness
Body	5¹³/₁₆″	3¹⁵/₁₆″	1⅜″
Right Front Leg	2¹/₁₆″	⁹/₁₆″	½″
Left Front Leg	2¹/₁₆″	⁹/₁₆″	½″
Right Hind Thigh	1″	1¼″	⅝″
Right Hind Leg	1¾″	¾″	⅜″
Left Hind Thigh	1″	1¼″	⅝″
Left Hind Leg	1¾″	¾″	⅜″

and a ¹/₁₆″ hole for the tail before attaching the legs. Size the end grain of the legs and glue them to the body. The head should face directly forward with no sideways tilt. The front and hind legs should be in alignment. Refer to Illus. 75–77 and Table 52 to complete the final shapes and details. The approximate carving time is 13 hours.

The following table provides the critical dimensions that you will need when carving a ⅛-scale or full-size model:

Table 52   Critical Dimensions for the Pig

	⅛ Scale	Full Size
Bottom of hind foot to top of ear	5⅝″	45″
Width of body at pole (includes corn)	1⅜″	11″
Width of rear flank	1³/₁₆″	9½″
Width of saddle at rear	1⅛″	9″
Width of head (excludes corn)	⅞″	7″
Width of nose	⅜″	3″
Distance between eyes	¹¹/₁₆″	5½″
Distance between tips of ears	¹⁵/₁₆″	7½″
Width of neck below head (includes corn)	1¼″	10″
Width of leg at body (front)	½″	4″
Width of leg at body (hind)	⅝″	5″
Width of leg at knee	⁵/₁₆″	2½″
Width of hoof	⅜″	3″
Length of hoof	⁷/₁₆″	3½″
Distance between front feet	⁷/₁₆″	3½″
Distance between hind feet	⁷/₁₆″	3½″
Width of tail (wire corkscrew)	¹/₁₆″	½″

After carving, paint as suggested by the color symbols or in colors you prefer. There are no jewels on this animal. To make the tail, bend a piece of ¹/₁₆″ diameter wire into a corkscrew and insert it into the hole in the rear of the body. Insert a 10¼″ length of ³/₁₆″ dowel through the hole in the body with 4″ above the saddle and glue it in place. Add the footrest (Illus. 5) to the pole. Make a stand and put the pole of the completed pig in the hole in the stand.

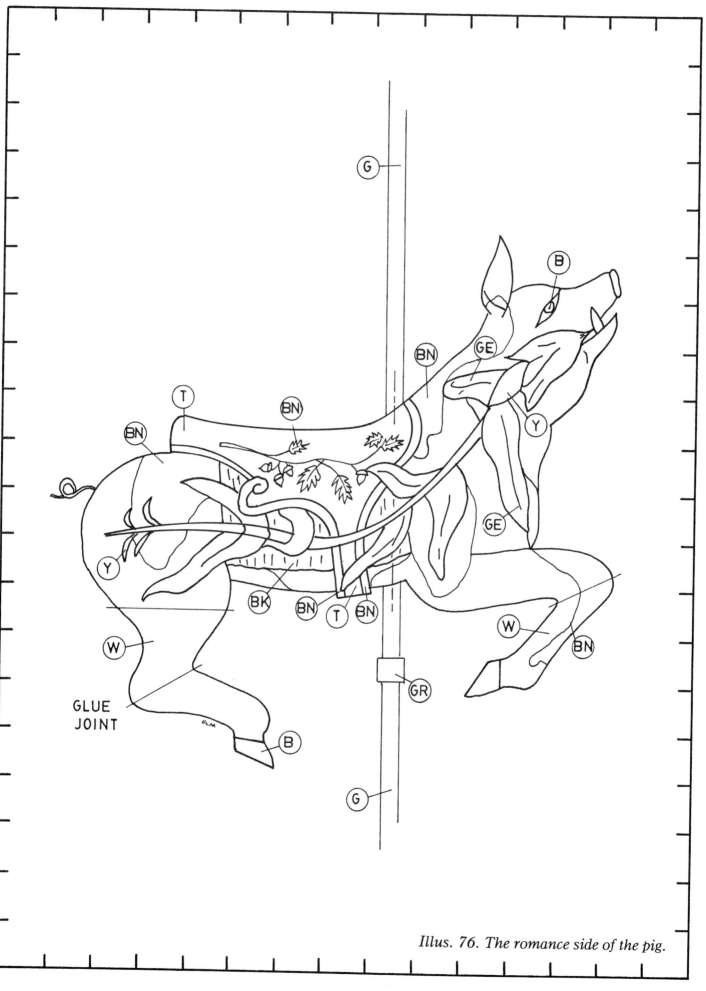

Illus. 76. The romance side of the pig.

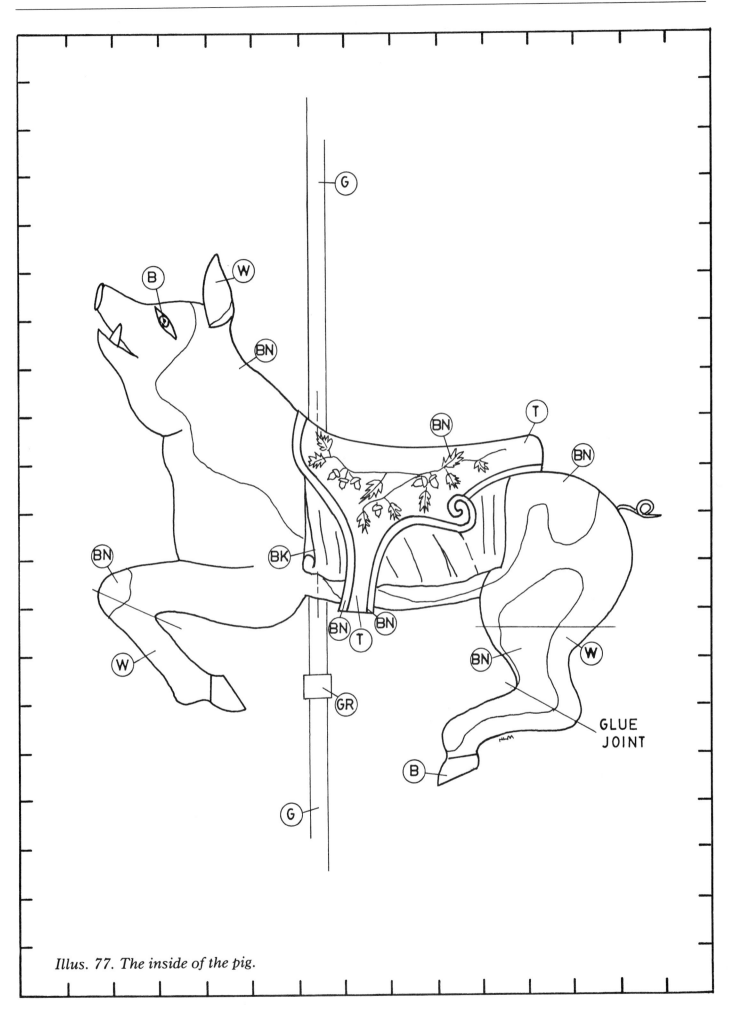

Illus. 77. The inside of the pig.

Zebra

Illus. 78. This animal is in its natural state and has no saddle or trappings of any kind. It is the least elaborate animal on the carousel. For a look at the zebra in full color, turn to page M of the Color Section.

DIRECTIONS

Using Illus. 79 as a plan, cut out the 16 patterns and glue each pattern to wood of the correct thickness as shown in Table 53. Refer to Illus. 80 for the complete pattern for the left hind leg. The length of each part should follow the direction of the grain.

The complete carving block consists of 16 parts, as follow: head, body, right front leg (3 sections), left front leg (3 sections), right hind leg (3 sections), left hind leg (3 sections), and tail (2 sections). Drill

Table 53   Parts List for the Zebra

Part	Length	Width	Thickness
Head	2¼″	1¼″	¾″
Body	5⁵⁄₁₆″	3¹⁄₁₆″	1³⁄₈″
Right Front Thigh	1⁵⁄₈″	¹⁵⁄₁₆″	½″
Right Front Leg	1³⁄₈″	⁷⁄₁₆″	³⁄₈″
Right Front Hoof	¹³⁄₁₆″	½″	⁷⁄₁₆″
Left Front Thigh	1⅛″	1¹⁄₁₆″	½″
Left Front Leg	1″	⁷⁄₁₆″	³⁄₈″
Left Front Hoof	¹³⁄₁₆″	½″	⁷⁄₁₆″
Right Hind Thigh	1⁵⁄₁₆″	1¼″	¹¹⁄₁₆″
Right Hind Leg	1⁵⁄₈″	⁵⁄₈″	³⁄₈″
Right Hind Hoof	⁵⁄₈″	½″	⁷⁄₁₆″
Left Hind Thigh	1⁵⁄₁₆″	1¼″	¹¹⁄₁₆″
Left Hind Leg	1⁵⁄₈″	⁵⁄₈″	³⁄₈″
Left Hind Hoof	⁵⁄₈″	½″	⁷⁄₁₆″
Tail (middle)	¾″	³⁄₈″	¼″
Tail (end)	1½″	½″	³⁄₈″

a ³⁄₁₆″ hole through the body before gluing the head and legs in place. Size the end grain of each piece and glue all of the parts in place. There is no sideways tilt to the head. Carve the head separately on this animal to give better grain direction, not to turn it. Place the pole between the ears. Refer to Illus. 78–80 and Table 54 when carving the final shape. The approximate carving time is 12 hours.

The following table provides the critical dimensions that you will need when carving a ⅛-scale or full-size model:

Table 54   Critical Dimensions for the Zebra

	⅛ Scale	Full Size
Bottom of hind foot to top of nose	7⁷⁄₁₆″	59½″
Width of body at pole	1⅛″	9″
Width of rear flank	1³⁄₈″	11″
Width of rear flank at tail	1¼″	10″
Width of chest	1³⁄₈″	11″
Width of head	¾″	6″
Width of nose	³⁄₈″	3″
Width of brush on top of head	⁵⁄₃₂″	1¼″
Distance between eyes	¹¹⁄₁₆″	5½″
Distance between tips of ears	¹¹⁄₁₆″	5½″
Width of neck at body	¾″	6″
Width of neck at head	½″	4″
Width of leg at body (front)	½″	4″
Width of leg at body (hind)	¹¹⁄₁₆″	5½″
Width of leg (thin areas)	¼″	2″
Width of leg at knee	⁵⁄₁₆″	2½″

Table continues on page 144

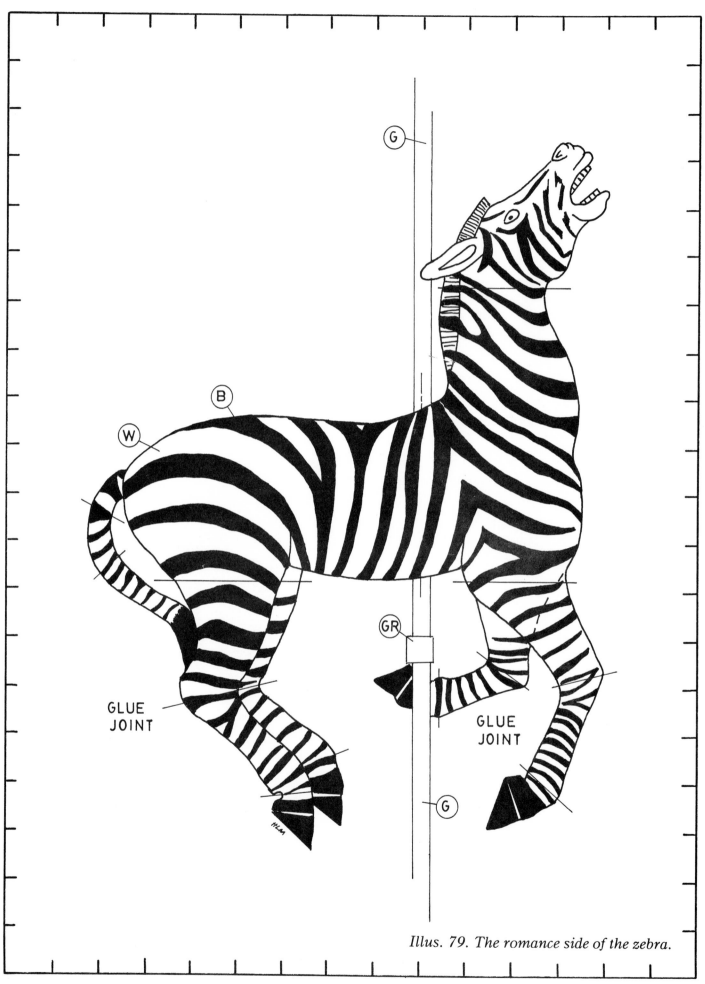

GLUE
JOINT

GLUE
JOINT

Illus. 79. The romance side of the zebra.

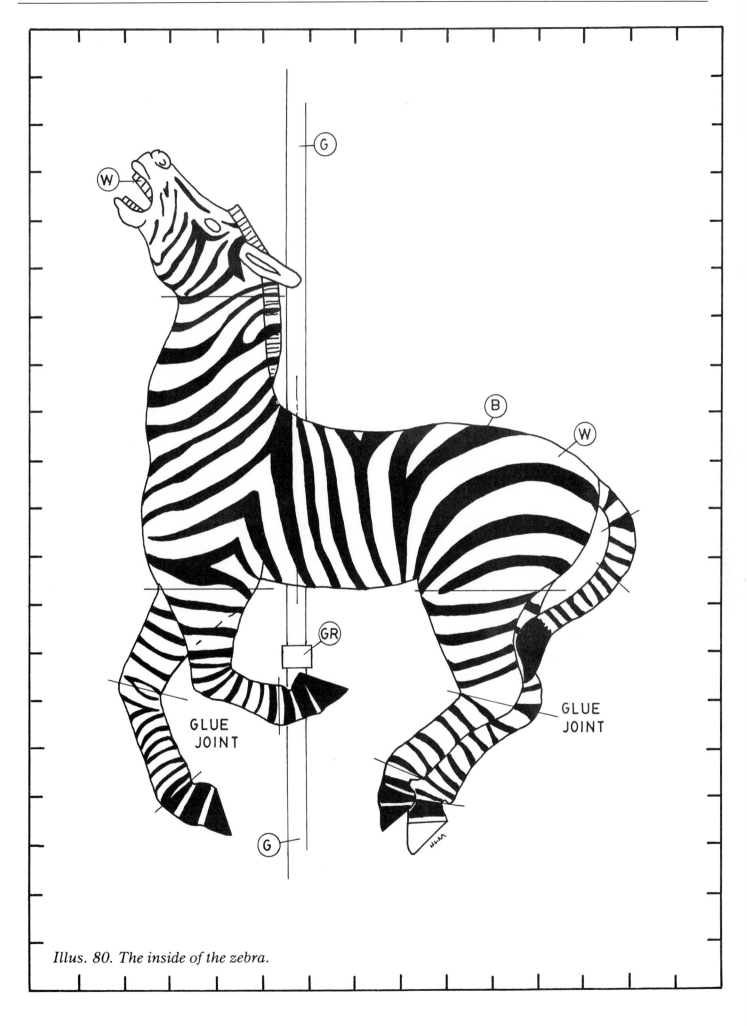

Illus. 80. The inside of the zebra.

	⅛ Scale	Full Size
Width of foot	⁷⁄₁₆″	3½″
Length of foot	⁹⁄₁₆″	4½″
Distance between front feet	⅝″	5″
Distance between hind feet	¾″	6″
Width of tail at body	¼″	2″
Width of tail at curve	³⁄₁₆″	1½″

After carving, paint as suggested by the color symbols. There are no jewels on this animal. Insert a 10¼″ length of ³⁄₁₆″ dowel through the hole in the body with 4″ above the saddle and glue it in place. Add the footrest (Illus. 5) to the pole. Make a stand and insert the pole of the completed zebra into it.

Black Beauty

GENERAL NOTES

This stunning horse, shown in Illus. 81 and 82, is highlighted with red trappings. With its front and hind legs in alignment, it gives the impression that it is bouncing up and down.

DIRECTIONS

Using Illus. 81 as a plan, cut out the 12 patterns and glue them to wood of the correct thickness as listed in Table 55. The length of each part should follow the direction of the grain.

Table 55   Parts List for Black Beauty

Part	Length	Width	Thickness
Head	1⅞″	1⅜″	¾″
Body	4¹⁵⁄₁₆″	2¾″	1¼″
Right Front Thigh	⅞″	1″	⅜″
Right Front Leg	1⁹⁄₁₆″	½″	⅜″
Left Front Thigh	⅞″	1″	⅜″
Left Front Leg	1⁹⁄₁₆″	½″	⅜″
Right Hind Thigh	1⅛″	1½″	⅝″
Right Hind Leg	1⁷⁄₁₆″	½″	⅜″
Right Hind Hoof	⅝″	⁷⁄₁₆″	⅜″
Left Hind Thigh	1⅛″	1½″	⅝″
Left Hind Leg	1⁷⁄₁₆″	½″	⅜″
Left Hind Hoof	⅝″	⁷⁄₁₆″	⅜″

The complete carving block is composed of 12 parts, as follow: head, body, right front leg (2 sections), left front leg (2 sections), right hind leg (3 sections), and left hind leg (3 sections). The head is turned approximately 5° to the right.

Drill a ³⁄₁₆″ hole through the body and a ⅛″ hole for the tail. Size the end grain of each leg part and glue the legs and head to the body. Cut out four horseshoes from ¹⁄₁₆″ stock and glue one to the bottom of each foot. Refer to Illus. 81 and 82 and Table 56 when carving the final shapes and details. The breast collar meets in the front, goes between the front legs, and joins the band from the saddle. Fasten an oval medallion to the very front. The approximate carving time is 12 hours.

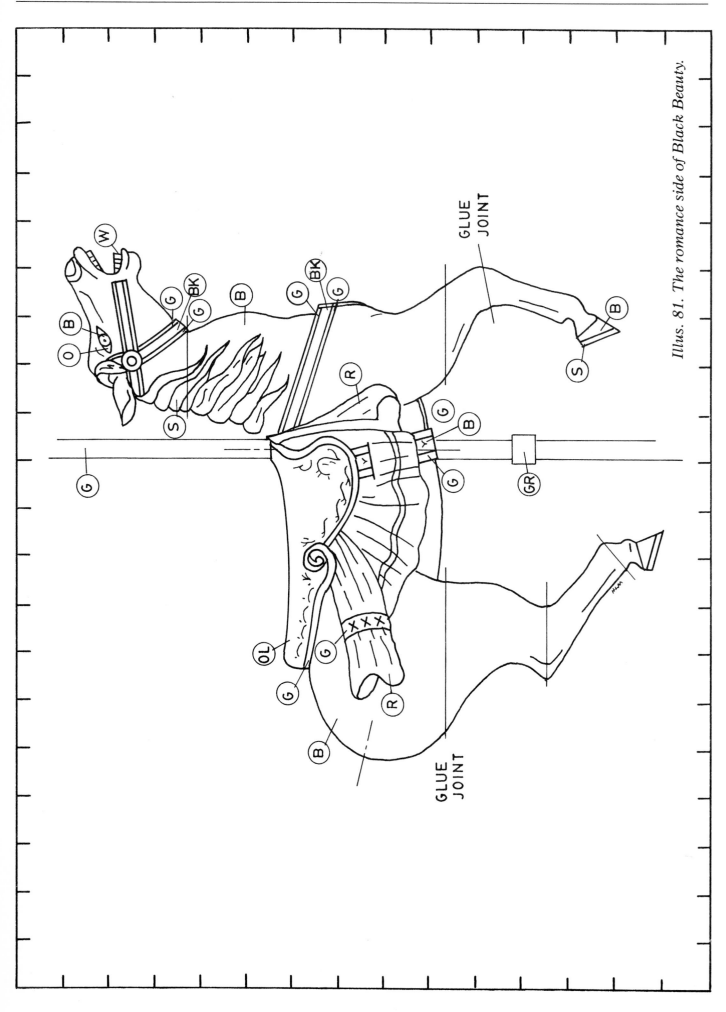

Illus. 81. The romance side of Black Beauty.

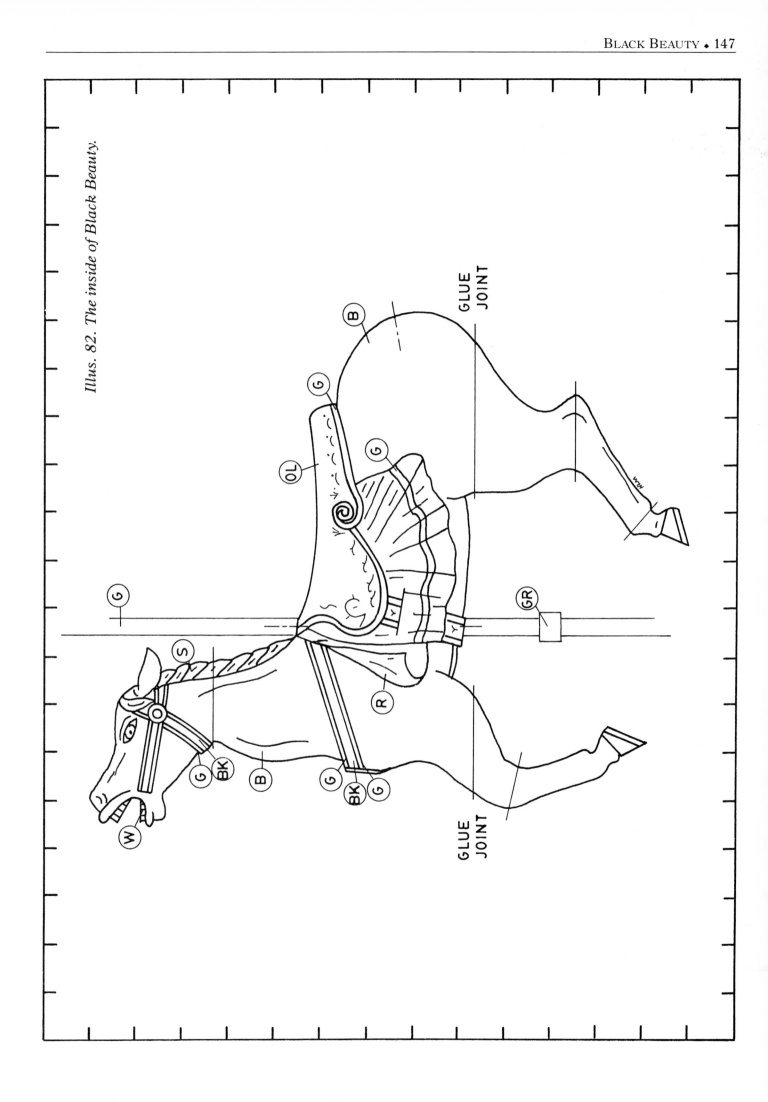

Illus. 82. The inside of Black Beauty.

The following table provides the critical dimensions that you will need when carving a ⅛-scale or full-size model:

Table 56   Critical Dimensions for Black Beauty

	⅛ Scale	Full Size
Distance from rear to chest	4¾″	38″
Width of head (including mane)	¾″	6″
Width of nose	13/32″	3¼″
Distance between eyes	11/16″	5½″
Distance between tips of ears	7/16″	3½″
Width of neck at breast collar	⅞″	7″
Width of neck at head	½″	4″
Width of body at pole	1 3/16″	9½″
Width of rear flank	1¼″	10″
Width of saddle at rear	1¼″	10″
Width of front leg at body	⅜″	3″
Width of hind leg at body	⅝″	5″
Width of leg at knee	¼″	2″
Width of hoof	⅜″	3″
Length of hoof	7/16″	3½″
Distance between front hooves	⅜″	3″
Distance between hind hooves	⅜″	3″

After doing the final carving and sanding, paint as suggested in Illus. 81 and 82. There are no jewels on this horse. Make the tail from approximately forty-five 2″ lengths of heavy-duty grey sewing thread. Insert a 10¼″ length of 3/16″ dowel through the body and glue it in place so that approximately 4″ extend above the saddle. Glue a footrest (Illus. 5) to the pole. Make a stand and glue the pole of the completed carving to it.

Cat

Illus. 83. The world is full of cat lovers, and on almost every carousel there is at least one domestic feline. For a look at the cat in full color, turn to page F of the Color Section.

DIRECTIONS

Using Illus. 84 as a plan, cut out the six patterns and glue each pattern to wood of the correct thickness as listed in Table 57. The length of each part should follow the direction of the grain.

The complete carving block consists of six parts, as follow: body, right hind leg (2 sections), left hind leg (2 sections), and the tail.

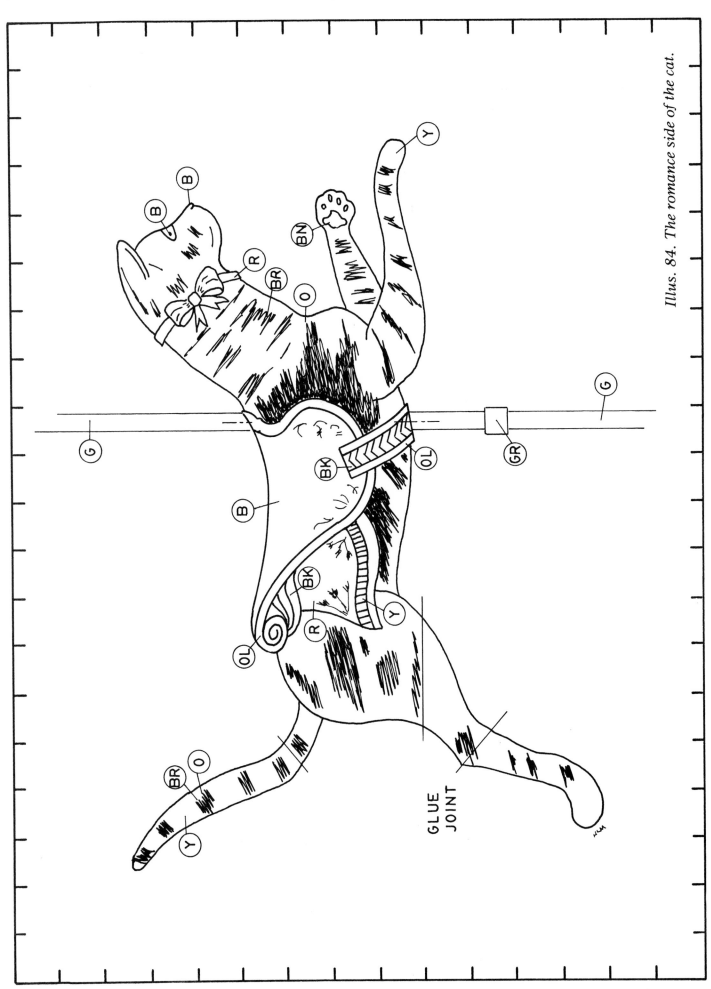

Illus. 84. The romance side of the cat.

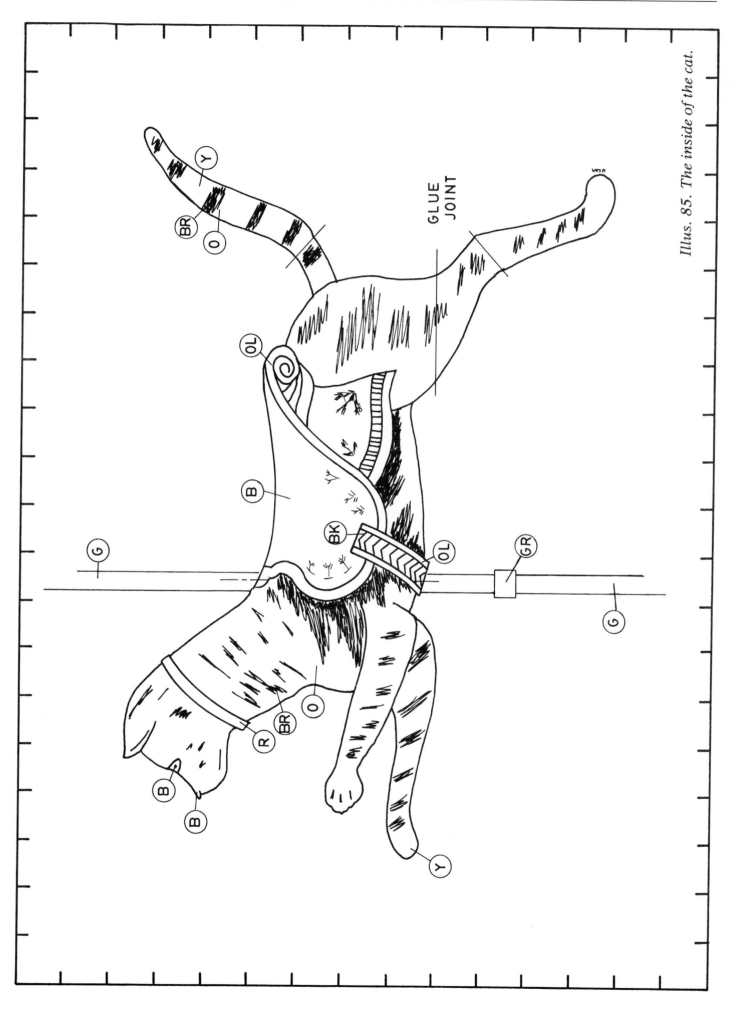

GLUE
JOINT

Illus. 85. The inside of the cat.

Table 57   Parts List for the Cat

Part	Length	Width	Thickness
Body	6⁹⁄₁₆″	3³⁄₈″	1¹⁄₁₆″
Right Hind Thigh	1³⁄₈″	³⁄₄″	½″
Right Hind Leg	1⁵⁄₈″	⁵⁄₈″	⁷⁄₁₆″
Left Hind Thigh	1³⁄₈″	³⁄₄″	½″
Left Hind Leg	1⁵⁄₈″	⁵⁄₈″	⁷⁄₁₆″
Tail	2⅛″	⁷⁄₁₆″	⁵⁄₁₆″

Drill a ³⁄₁₆″ hole through the body before attaching the legs. Size all the end grain and glue the legs and tail to the body. There is no sideways tilt to the head. The romance side and the inside are identical except for the bow on the neck. The hind legs should be in alignment. The left front paw should be turned so that the pad is vertical. Refer to Illus. 83–85 and Table 58 for final details and shapes. The approximate carving time is 12 hours.

The following table provides the critical dimensions that you will need when carving a ⅛-scale or full-size model:

Table 58   Critical Dimensions for the Cat

	⅛ Scale	Full Size
Bottom of hind foot to top of ear	5⁵⁄₁₆″	42½″
Width of body at pole	1¹⁄₁₆″	8½″
Width of rear flank	1″	8″
Width of saddle at rear	1″	8″
Width of chest	1¹⁄₁₆″	8½″
Width of head	1³⁄₃₂″	8³⁄₄″
Width of nose	⅛″	1″
Distance between eyes	½″.	4″
Distance between tips of ears	¹³⁄₁₆″	6½″
Width of neck at body	¹⁵⁄₁₆″	7½″
Width of leg at body (front)	³⁄₈″	3″
Width of leg at body (hind)	½″	4″
Width of leg at knee	¼″	2″
Width of paw	⁷⁄₁₆″	3½″
Length of paw	½″	4″
Distance between front paws	⁷⁄₁₆″	3½″
Distance between hind paws	³⁄₈″	3″
Width of tail at body	⁵⁄₁₆″	2½″
Width of tail at tip	³⁄₁₆″	1½″
Length of tail	2¼″	18″

After carving, follow the suggested color symbols to paint the carving or select colors that you prefer. There are no jewels on this animal. Insert a 10¼″ length of ³⁄₁₆″ dowel through the hole in the body with 4¼″ extending above the saddle. Glue it in place and add the footrest (Illus. 5) to the pole. Make a stand and glue the pole of the completed cat to it.

Frog

Illus. 86. This carousel animal is the only one ever carved wearing human clothing. It is believed that the creator was influenced by Kenneth Grahame's book entitled Wind in the Willows. *For a look at the frog in full color, turn to page E of the Color Section.*

DIRECTIONS

Using Illus. 87 as a plan, cut out the five patterns and adhere each pattern to wood of the correct thickness as listed in Table 59. The length of each part should follow the direction of the grain.

The complete carving block consists of five parts, as follow: body, right leg (2 sections), and left leg (2 sections). Drill a ³⁄₁₆″ hole through the body before attaching the legs. Size the end grain and glue the legs to the body. There is no sideways tilt to the head. The only difference between the romance side and the inside is that there are buttons on the romance side and buttonholes on the inside.

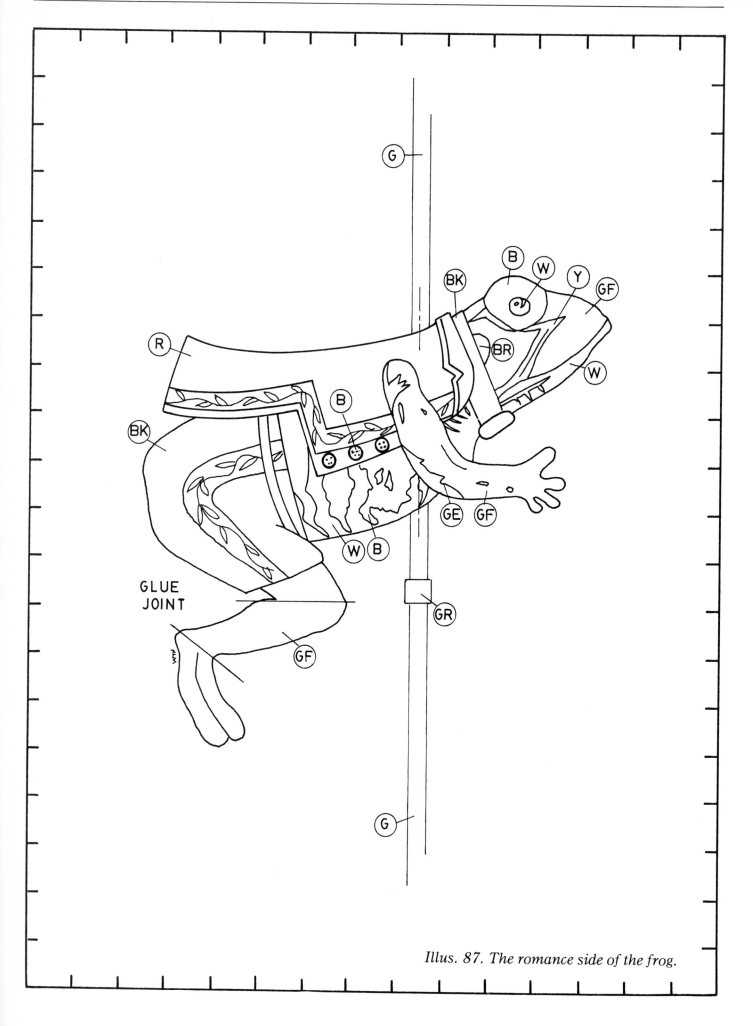

Illus. 87. The romance side of the frog.

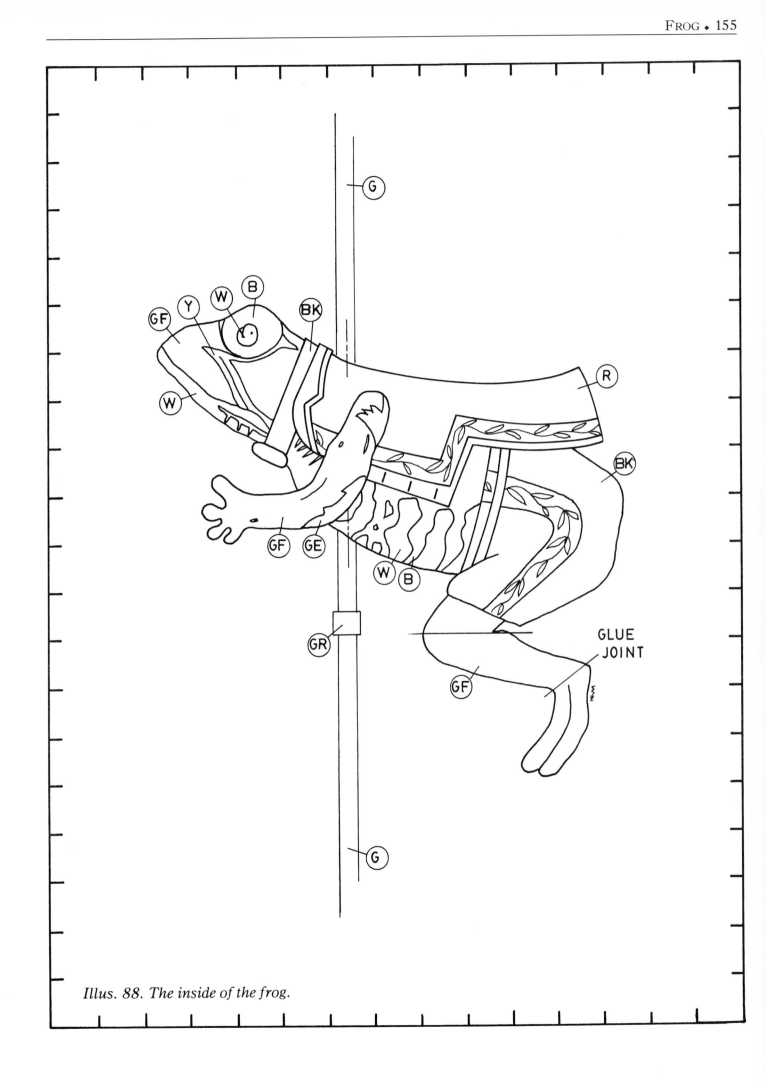

Illus. 88. The inside of the frog.

Table 59 Parts List for the Frog

Part	*Length*	*Width*	*Thickness*
Body	5⅛″	3⅜″	1⅝″
Right Leg	1⅞″	½″	½″
Right Foot	1⅜″	9/16″	⅝″
Left Leg	1⅞″	½″	½″
Left Foot	1⅜″	9/16″	⅝″

Make sure that the legs and front paws are in alignment. Carve the buttons from the body or drill three ⅛″ holes ¼″ deep and insert a 5/16″ length of ⅛″ dowel in each hole. Cut in the arms; they should appear as if they are coming through the vest.

Raise the collar on the front of the jacket. Spread the legs wider at the feet than at the knees. To complete the final shapes and details, see Illus. 86–88 and Table 60. The approximate carving time is 14 hours.

The following table provides the critical dimensions that you will need when carving a ⅛-scale or full-size model:

Table 60 Critical Dimensions for the Frog

	⅛ Scale	*Full Size*
Bottom of foot to top of eye	5″	40″
Width of body at pole	1⅜″	11″
Width of rear flank	1⅜″	11″
Width of saddle at rear	1 5/16″	10½″
Width of arms at pole	1⅝″	13″
Width of head at eyes	1″	8″
Width of nose	7/16″	3½″
Distance between eyes	1″	8″
Width of neck	1″	8″
Width of front paw	¼″	2″
Width of leg at body	½″	4″
Width of leg at knee	7/16″	3½″
Width of foot at ankle	¼″	2″
Width of foot	⅝″	5″
Length of foot	1¼″	10″
Distance between front paws	½″	4″
Width of buttocks	⅝″	5″

After carving, paint in the colors suggested or select those you prefer. You can apply the lines on the jacket and pants very effectively by using paint with a draftsman's ruling pen. There are no jewels on the frog. Insert a 10¼″ length of 3/16″ dowel through the hole in the body so that 4½″ extend above the coat. Glue it in place and add the footrest (Illus. 5). Make a stand and place the pole of the completed frog in it.

Dog

Illus. 89. No carousel would be complete without a dog—another domestic favorite. For a look at the dog in full color, turn to page E of the Color Section.

DIRECTIONS

Using Illus. 90 as a plan, cut out the six patterns and adhere each pattern to wood of the correct thickness as shown in Table 61. The length of each part should follow the direction of the grain.

The complete carving block consists of six parts, as follow: body, right front leg, right hind leg, left hind leg (2 sections) and tail. Drill a 3/16" hole through the body before attaching the legs. Size the end

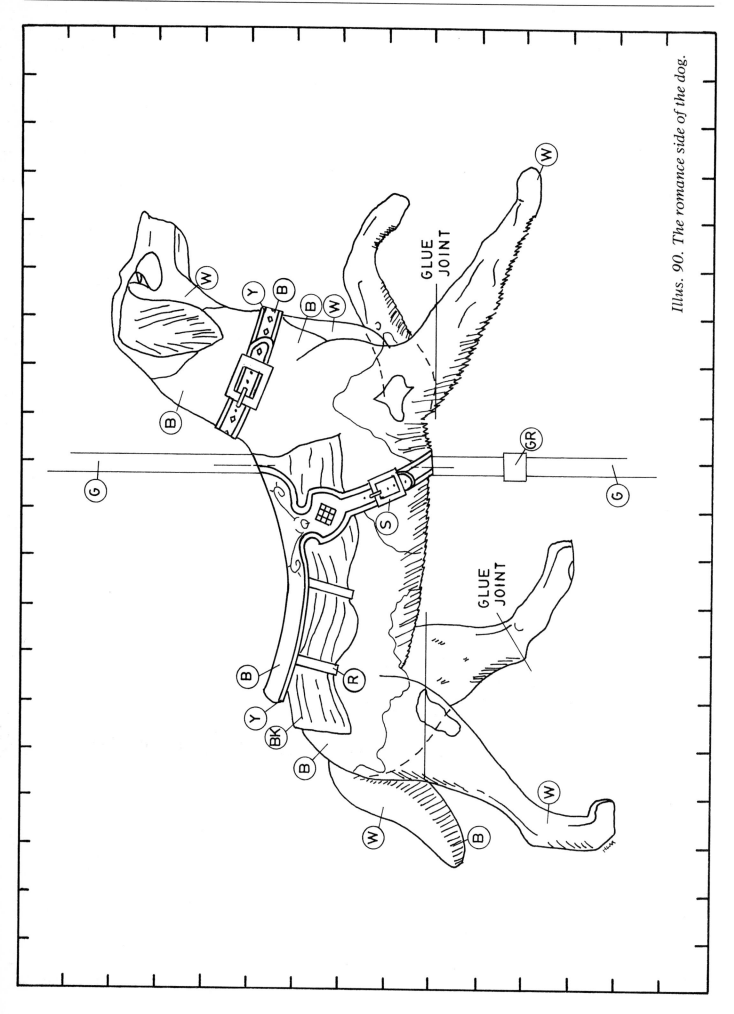

Illus. 90. The romance side of the dog.

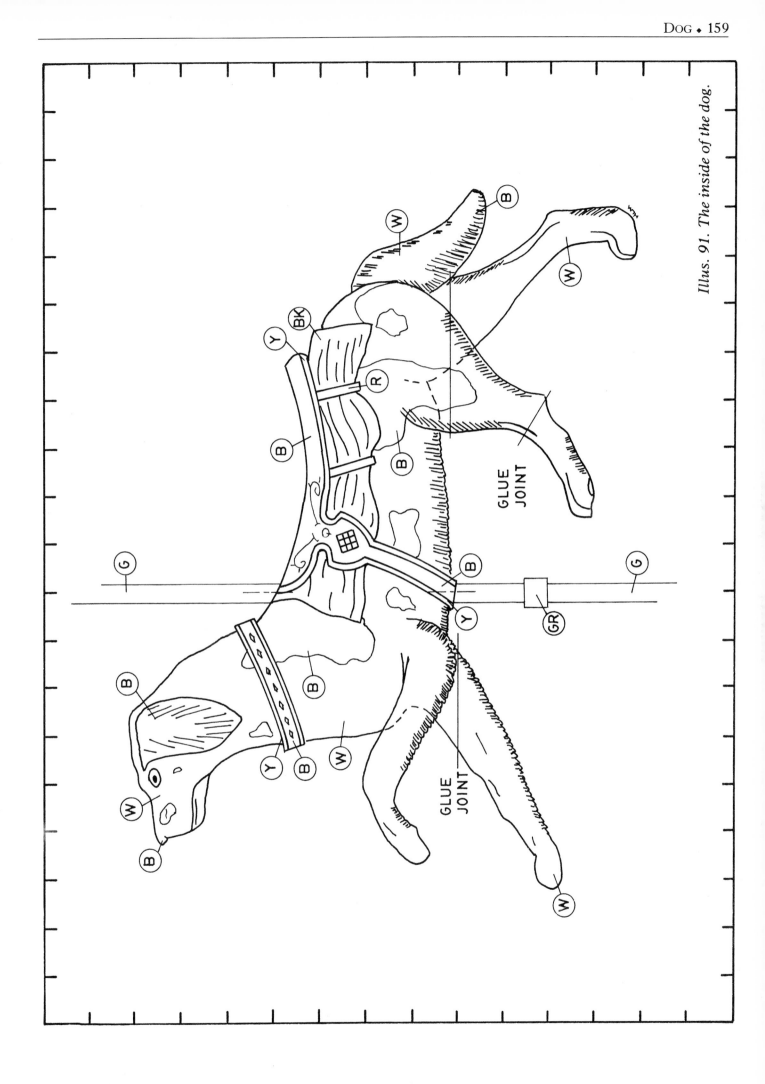

Illus. 91. The inside of the dog.

Table 61   Parts List for the Dog

Part	Length	Width	Thickness
Body	6⅛″	3½″	1¼″
Right Front Leg	2¹³⁄₁₆″	⅝″	⁷⁄₁₆″
Right Hind Leg	2½″	⅞″	⁷⁄₁₆″
Left Hind Thigh	1⅜″	1¹⁄₁₆″	⁷⁄₁₆″
Left Hind Leg	1⅜″	½″	⁷⁄₁₆″
Tail	1¹³⁄₁₆″	¾″	⁵⁄₁₆″

grain and glue the legs and tail to the body. The head should face directly ahead without any sideways tilt. The romance side and inside are identical with the exception of the buckles. Refer to Illus. 89–91 and Table 62 when carving the final shapes and details. The approximate carving time is 13 hours.

The following table provides the critical dimensions that you will need when carving a ⅛-scale or full-size model:

Table 62   Critical Dimensions for the Dog

	⅛ Scale	Full Size
Bottom of right hind paw to top of head	5⅝″	45″
Width of body at pole	1⅛″	9″
Width of rear flank	1″	8″
Width of saddle at rear	1¹⁄₁₆″	8½″
Width of breast	1¼″	10″
Width of head at ears	1¹⁄₁₆″	8½″
Width of nose	½″	4″
Distance between eyes	⁷⁄₁₆″	3½″
Width of neck at belt	1″	8″
Width of leg at body (front)	⁷⁄₁₆″	3½″
Width of leg at body (hind)	⁷⁄₁₆″	3½″
Width of leg at knee	¼″	2″
Width of paw	⁷⁄₁₆″	3½″
Length of paw	⅜″	3″
Distance between front paws	⅜″	3″
Distance between hind paws	⅜″	3″
Width of tail	⁵⁄₁₆″	2½″

After carving, paint in the colors suggested or select ones that you prefer. It is difficult to paint the series of diamonds on the collar even with a tiny brush. One alternative is to paint a piece of white paper, cut out the diamonds, and glue them to the collar. You can make the ³⁄₁₆″ square on the side of the saddle the same way. Use a ruling pen and ink in the lines before gluing the square to the saddle. There are no jewels on the dog.

Insert a 10¼″ length of ³⁄₁₆″ dowel through the hole in the body with 5″ above the saddle. Glue it in place and add the footrest (Illus. 5) to the pole. Make a stand and put the pole of the completed carving into the hole drilled into the stand.

FULL-SIZE
CAROUSEL ANIMALS

Carving the Full-Size Carousel Animal

he basic steps for carving a scale-size carousel animal, as outlined on pages 12–20, apply equally well to carving the full-size animal. The major differences are the size of the blocks, the carving tools, and the amount of time involved.

HOW TO ENLARGE THE PLAN

The first step is to select the animal. If a plan has to be created, follow the suggestions presented on pages 12 and 13 under the heading "Developing the Plan."

The second step is to determine the size. Do you want the animal full size or something less than full size? Many homes and apartments have limited space, so there may not be sufficient room for a full-size carving.

After you have determined the most appropriate size, develop a pattern to meet the size specification. Let's use the lead horse (pages 22–26) as an example, and enlarge the plan to full size. This would be an enlargement of eight magnitudes—from one-eighth scale to full size.

Connect the top to bottom grid points and left to right grid points. The lead-horse plan will now be covered with a series of ½" squares. Each square will be equal to 4" on the full-size animal. Secure large sheets of white paper from an art dealer and glue them together with rubber cement to form one sheet 56" wide × 60" high. Rule the sheet into four-inch squares. Start at the lower left corner and designate each line. Let the corner represent 0 (zero) and number the vertical lines 1 to 14. Letter the horizontal lines A to O.

To make the full-size pattern, follow the grid on the scale plan and transfer each line to the same relative position on the larger sheet. This procedure is referred to as enlarging by the "square" method, and is illustrated in Illus. 93. For example, the curve of the rear flank starts at H 1. It crosses G just to the right of point G 1, and proceeds to cross F between points F 1 and F 2. The line continues to the intersection of E 2 and crosses D to the left of D 2. Follow this procedure until the entire scale plan is enlarged and transferred to the larger sheet.

Scale plans can also be enlarged with a pantograph. The size of the enlargement will be limited by the length of the arm on the pantograph. It is possible to make the enlargement in a series of steps, but this would be time-consuming and the chance for error is increased. For the full-size plans, the square method is the best option.

MAKING THE TEMPLATES

Using the full-size plan, separate it into 12 patterns as follow: head, neck, body, right front leg (3 pieces), left front leg, right hind leg (3 pieces), and left hind leg (2 pieces). Each part (with the exception of the head) will have a mortise, tenon, or both. The tenons, as detailed in Illus. 94–99, must be added to the pattern.

Glue or trace the patterns—including the tenons—onto non-corrugated cardboard. Cut out the outline of each part to form the templates that will be used to transfer the pattern to the wood.

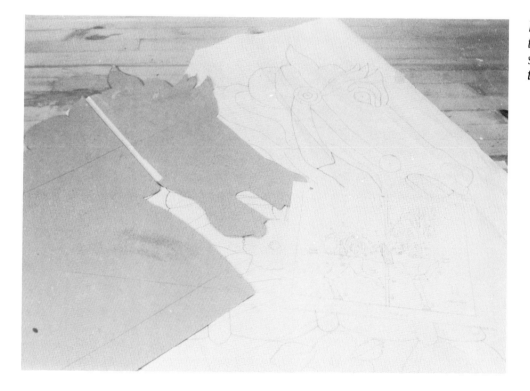

Illus. 92. Shown here are the scale drawing, the full-size plan, and a cardboard template.

LAMINATING THE CARVING BLOCK

This full-size lead horse has a hollow body to reduce the weight and amount of wood required; even so, it will require approximately 95 board feet of basswood. Because of the size, the seven carving blocks should each be laminated, carved separately, and then assembled.

The parts to be cut out and laminated for each block are shown in Illus. 95–98. All of the dimensions are for stock with a finish

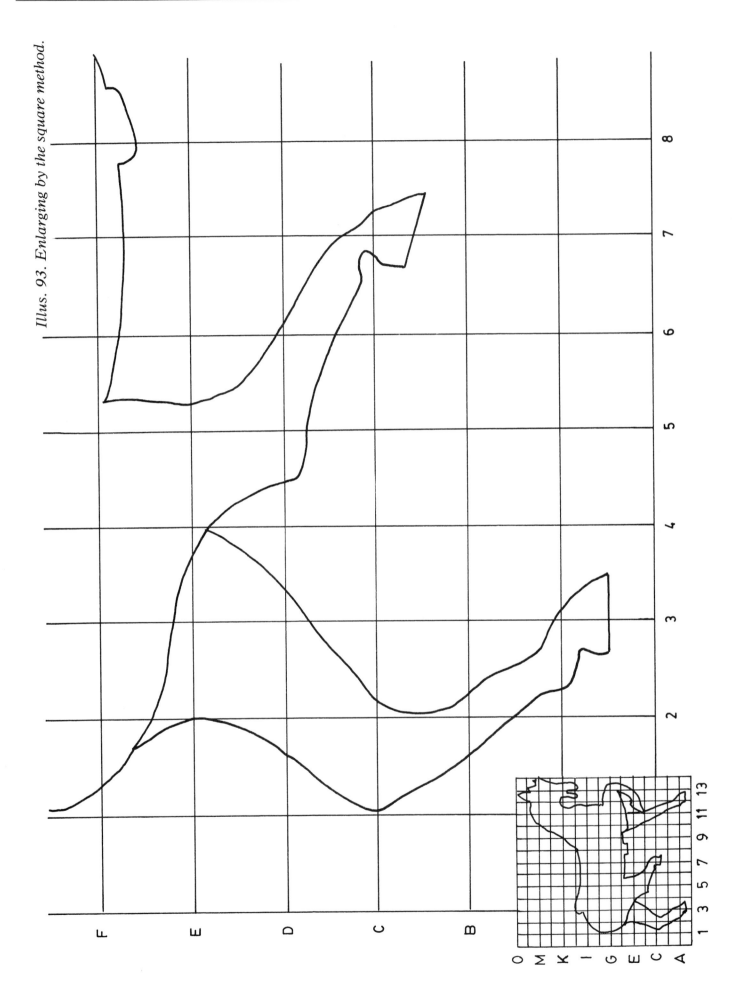

Illus. 93. Enlarging by the square method.

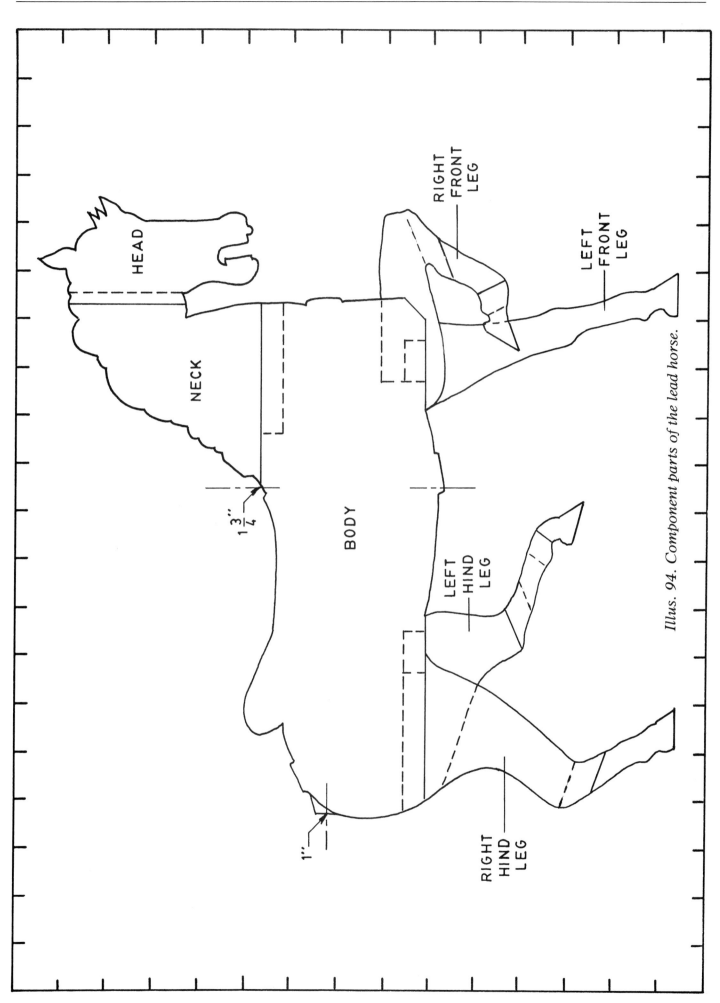

Illus. 94. Component parts of the lead horse.

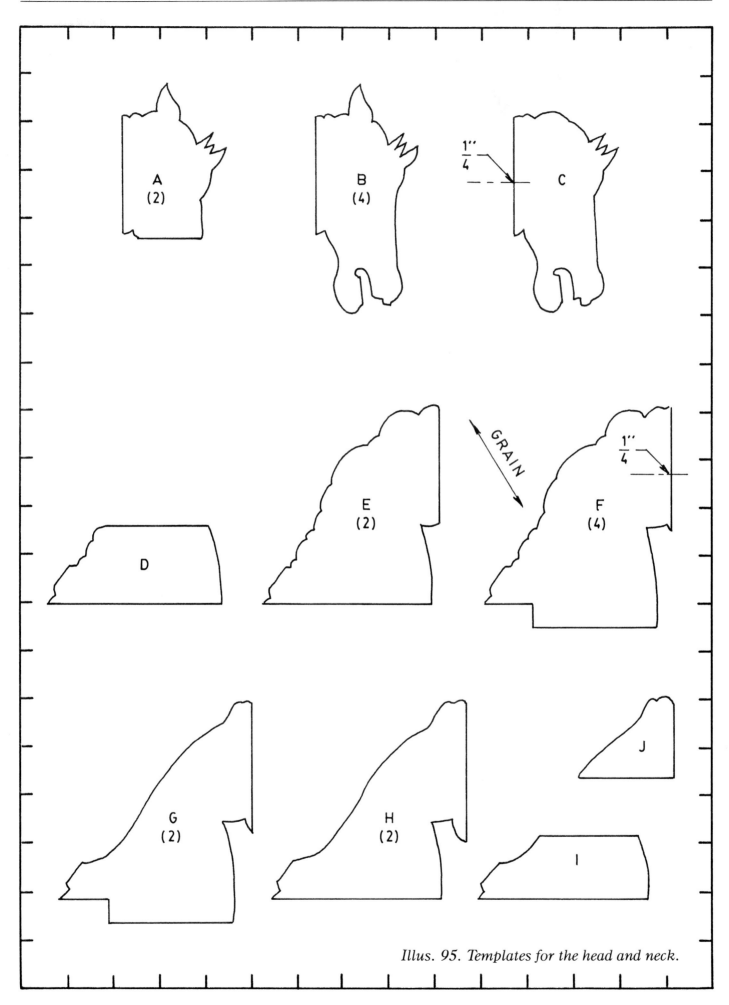

Illus. 95. Templates for the head and neck.

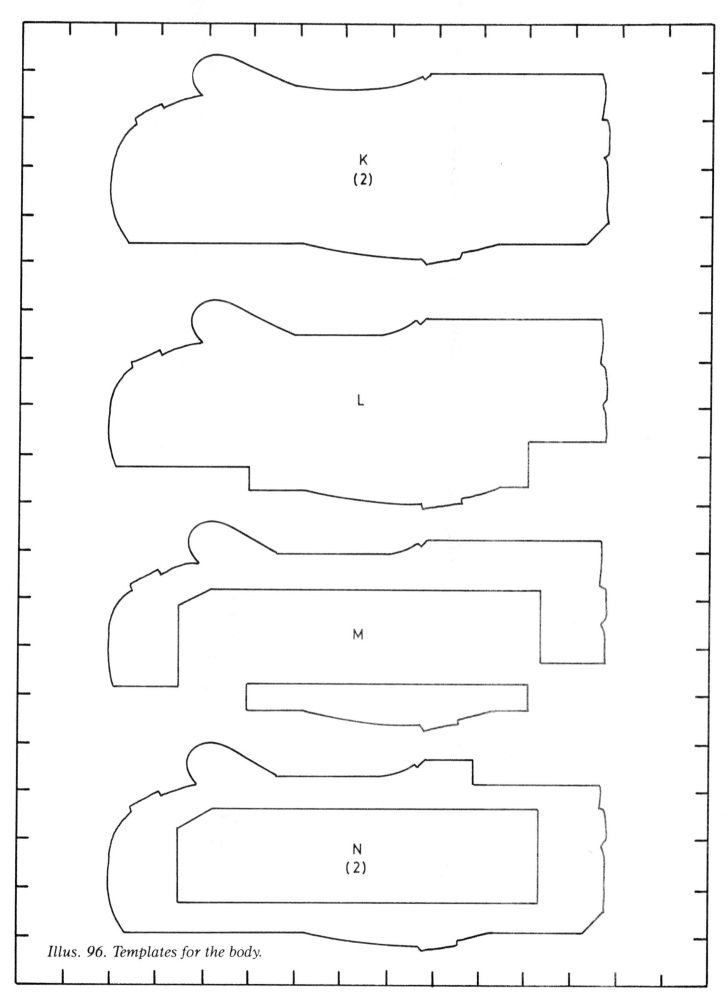

Illus. 96. Templates for the body.

K
(2)

L

M

N
(2)

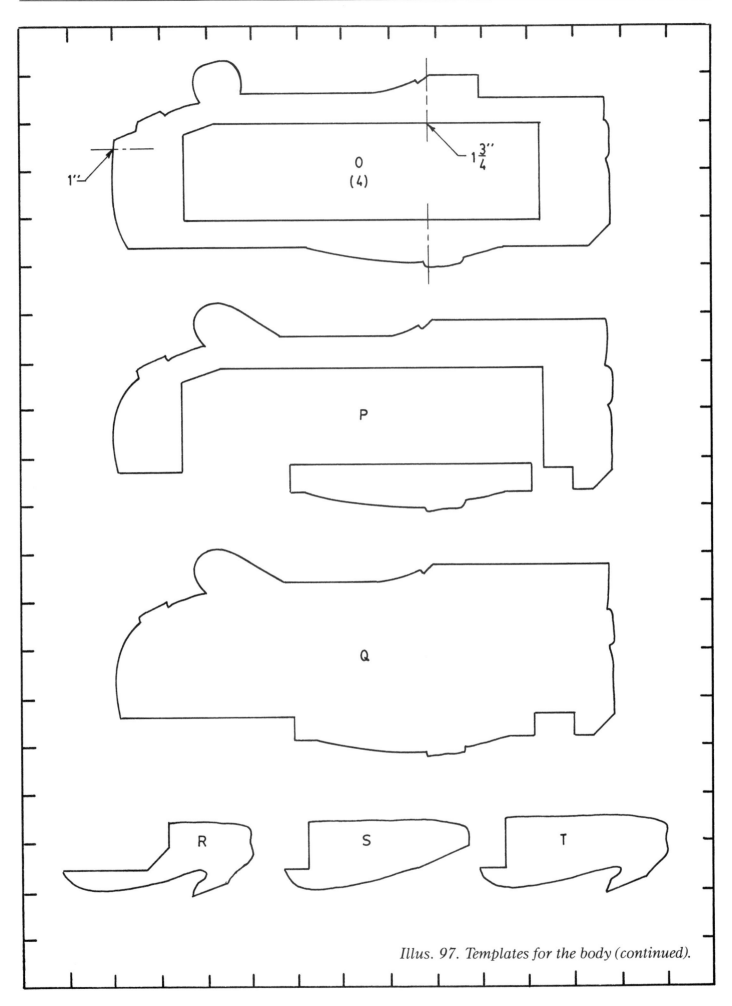

Illus. 97. Templates for the body (continued).

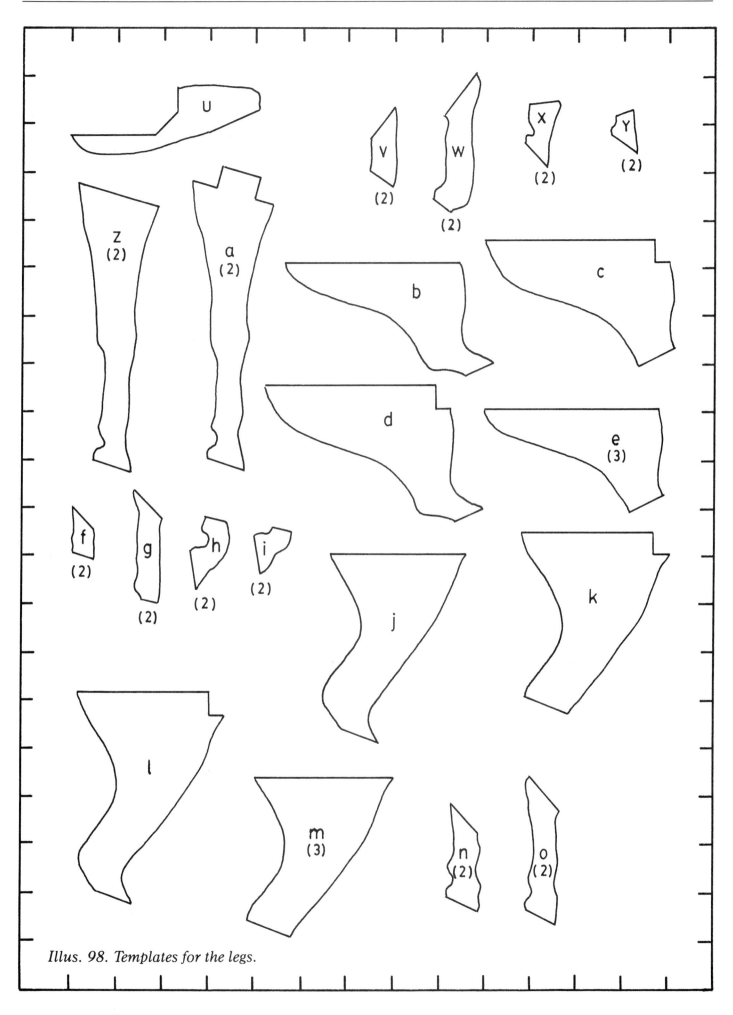

Illus. 98. Templates for the legs.

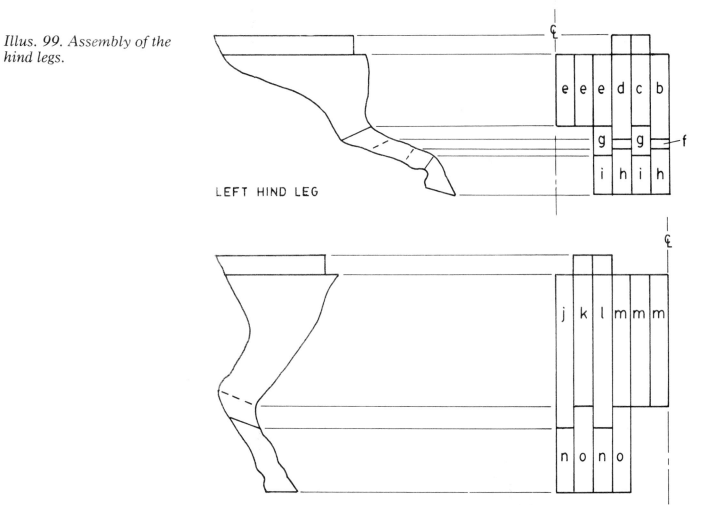

Illus. 99. Assembly of the hind legs.

LEFT HIND LEG

RIGHT HIND LEG

Illus. 100. A laminate part being roughed out on the band saw.

thickness of 1″. If you are using thicker stock, you can combine the patterns. For example, you will glue 12 segments together with 1″ stock to achieve the total width of the body. This could be reduced to six segments if 2″ stock is used, although modifications to the patterns and the mortises and tenons of some parts will be necessary. As already noted, the parts are held together by mortise-and-tenon joints. Dowels may be inserted at the joints to add greater stability, but if you are careful in fitting and gluing the joint, they will not be necessary.

Lay out each part so that the annual rings alternate as shown in Illus. 101. The gluing suggestions provided on page 13 also apply here. You will need a supply of large C-clamps, furniture clamps,

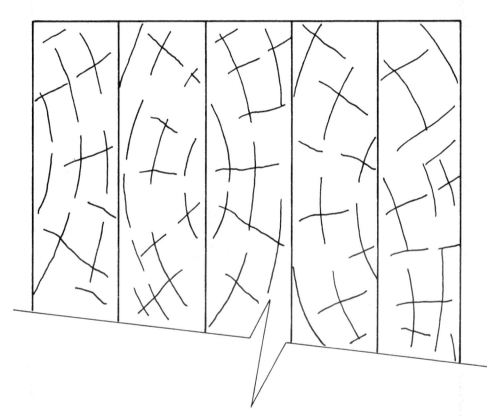

Illus. 101. Direction of annual rings.

Illus. 102. Laminated parts being held in place by pipe clamp for gluing.

clamping straps, or very heavy weights to hold each laminate as it is being glued. Do not attempt to glue all the laminates together at one time.

It is strongly recommended that you do a scale mock-up of each carving block before laminating the full-size blocks. To do this, use Illus. 95–98 as patterns (use as printed, do not enlarge) and cut each piece from ⅛" thick stock. Glue the pieces together to form the seven carving blocks as detailed below, and make sure that each part fits properly. This scale mock-up will help you visualize the entire project, show you how each block fits, and minimize the chance of error when you cut the full-size parts. Illus. 103 shows the disassembled mock-up for the lead horse, and Illus. 104 shows the assembled mock-up.

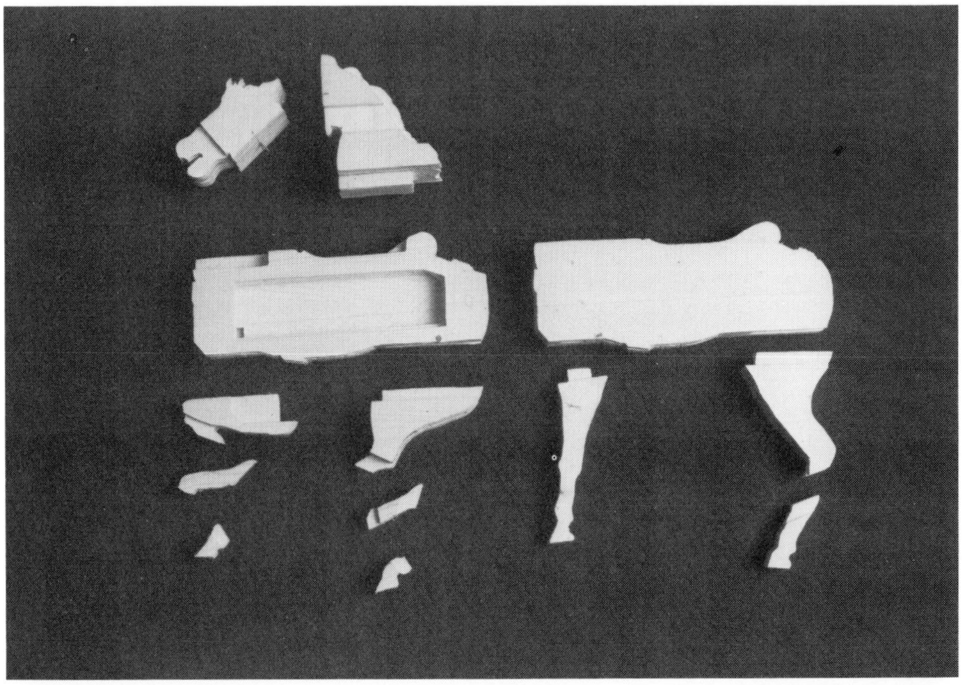

Illus. 103. Disassembled mock-up of the lead horse.

Illus. 104. Assembled mock-up of the lead horse.

Head

The head is made up of seven pieces and uses three templates (Illus. 95). Cut out the pieces with a band saw. Drill a ¼″ hole ¼″ deep into piece C, as shown in Illus. 95. Assemble the pieces in the following order to form the head carving block: A, B, B, C, B, B, A. This is the only block that has no mortise or tenon.

Neck

The neck is made up of 13 pieces and requires seven templates (Illus. 95). Note the diagonal direction of the grain. Cut out the pieces with a band saw. Imagine that you are standing in front of and facing the horse. Assemble the pieces in the following order: D, E, E, F, F, F, F, G, G, H, H, I/J. Piece D will be on your left and pieces I/J on the extreme right.

After the glue has thoroughly dried, cut a bevel on the front surface where the head will be glued. Measure ½″ in from the front edge of piece E and draw a line parallel to the front edge. From the point where this line touches the top of E, draw a line to the front edge at the top of J. Remove the wood in front of this line so that the front surface of the neck is straight but sloping towards the romance side. Drill a ¼″ hole on the centerline as noted on piece F.

Body

The body is made up of 12 pieces, requires seven patterns, and constitutes the largest carving block (Illus. 96 and 97). Cut out all of the pieces. Assemble the body in two halves. Work in the same position as explained for assembling the neck and assemble the romance side in the following order: K, L, M, N, O, O, ₵. Assemble the inside half in this order: ₵, O, O, N, P, Q, K. The O pieces will meet at the centerline. Glue the two halves together.

Drill a 1″ hole 2″ deep on the centerline for the tail as noted on template O. Drill a 1¾″ hole (for the pole) on the centerline through the top and bottom of the O pieces as noted on template O.

Right Front Leg

The right front leg is made up of 12 pieces which are assembled into three parts—thigh, leg, and hoof (Illus. 97 and 98). It will be necessary to make eight templates. Cut out all of the pieces. Work in the same position as explained for assembling the neck and assemble the thigh in the following order: R, S, T, U. Assemble the leg in the following order: V, W, V, W. Assemble the hoof in this order: X, Y, X, Y. Join together the thigh, leg, and hoof to form the total carving block for this leg.

Left Front Leg

The left front leg is made up of four pieces and requires two templates (Illus. 98). Cut out the pieces and assemble them in this order: Z, a, a, Z.

Right Hind Leg

The right hind leg is made up of ten pieces, requires six templates, and is assembled in two parts—the thigh and leg (Illus. 98 and 99). Cut the ten pieces to shape. Work in the same position as explained for assembling the neck and assemble the thigh in the following order: j, k, l, m, m, m, ₵. Assemble the leg in the following order: n, o, n, o. Join the thigh and leg together to form the complete carving block for this leg.

Left Hind Leg

The left hind leg is made up of 14 pieces, requires eight templates, and is assembled in three parts—the thigh, leg, and hoof (Illus. 98 and 99). Work in the same position as previously explained and assemble the thigh in the following order: ₵, e, e, e, d, c, b. Assemble the leg in the order of g, f, g, f, and the hoof in the order of i, h, i, h. Join the thigh, leg, and hoof together to form the complete carving block for this leg.

HORSESHOES

Make four horseshoes. Each shoe should be made of three layers (five parts), as shown in Illus. 106. Cut part A from $5/16''$ stock and part B from $3/16''$ stock. Cut out two part C's and one part D from $1/8''$ stock. Glue part B on top of part A. Glue a part C to each side of the open end and glue part D to the center of the horseshoe. When the glue is dry, use a round file or coarse sandpaper wrapped around a $1/4''$ dowel to "blend" parts C and D to part B. Sand the entire horseshoe. Size the bottom of each hoof (end grain) and glue one horseshoe to each hoof.

Illus. 105. Finished horseshoe glued in place and ready for final leg carvings.

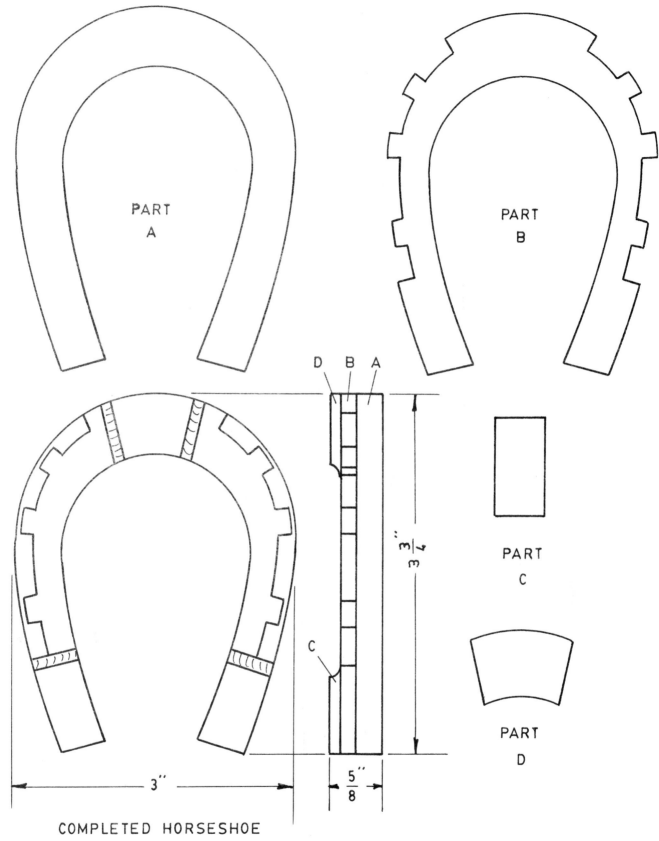

PART
A

PART
B

D B A

PART
C

C

3
3/4

COMPLETED HORSESHOE

3"

5/8"

PART
D

Illus. 106. Horseshoe patterns.

CARVING AND ASSEMBLY

The blocks will be easier to handle if you completely carve and sand each of them before assembling them. Complete all of the details on each block except the areas where the blocks will be joined. Do the final carving in these areas after the parts have been joined.

Carve the head and neck and finish-sand. Insert a ½″ length of ¼″ dowel in the hole in the head and glue the head to the neck. The centerline of the head should be at a 33° angle to the centerline of the neck (Illus. 112).

Carve the body, and then join the body and neck. Place the body on sawhorses and, after carving the legs, glue the legs to the body in the following order: front right leg, left hind leg, right hind leg, and front left leg.

The actual carving time will vary with the ability and experience of the carver. In general, a full-size animal will require approximately ten times longer to carve than the one-eighth scale model. Additional time will be required to make the plan, glue up the blocks, and do the painting.

As a guide to aid in your planning, remember that approximately 60 hours are required to develop the plans and build the scale model for the lead horse, 87 hours to cut and glue up the blocks, 263 hours to actually carve and assemble the pieces, 57 hours to sand, and 65 hours to paint.

You will have to consult Table 3 for critical dimensions when carving this full-size carousel lead horse. The following guidelines will prove helpful when you are carving: The saddle is raised ¾″ above the horse's body. The depressions in the mane are approximately 3″ deep. The ears are hollow, with the openings towards the rear. There are eight teeth, top and bottom, and each tooth is approximately as high as it is wide. The front of the neck is tapered and is at its widest where it meets the ribbon.

Refer to Illus. 111 (romance side) and Illus. 112–114 when carving the full-size lead horse.

Illus. 107. Mortise-and-tenon method of joining the neck to the body.

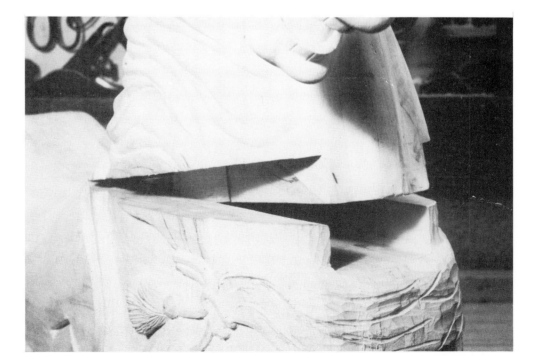

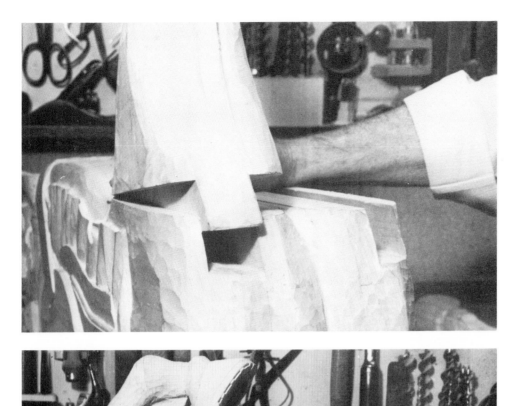

Illus. 108. Joining the hind legs to the body. Note that the tenon is part of the rump.

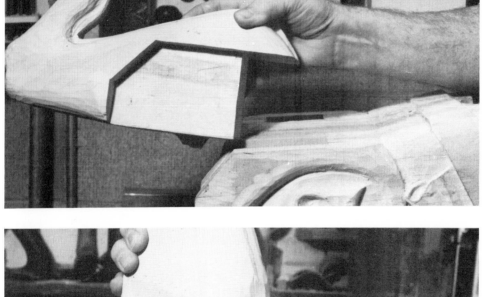

Illus. 109. Joining the right front leg to the body.

Illus. 110. Joining the left front leg to the body.

Illus. 111. Romance side of the lead horse.

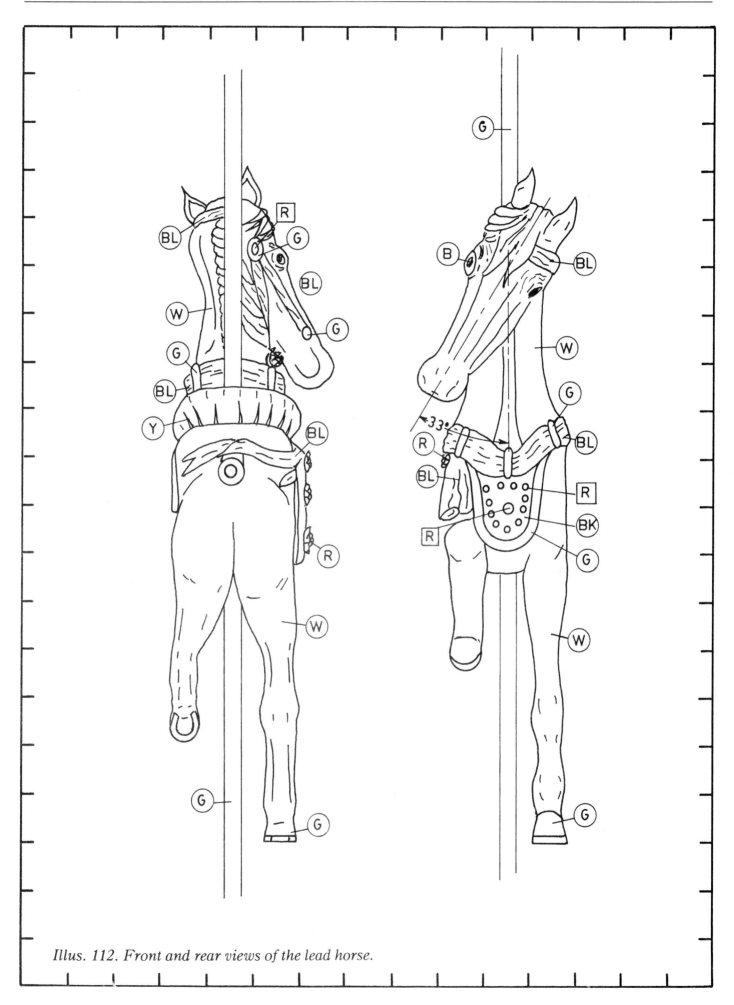

Illus. 112. Front and rear views of the lead horse.

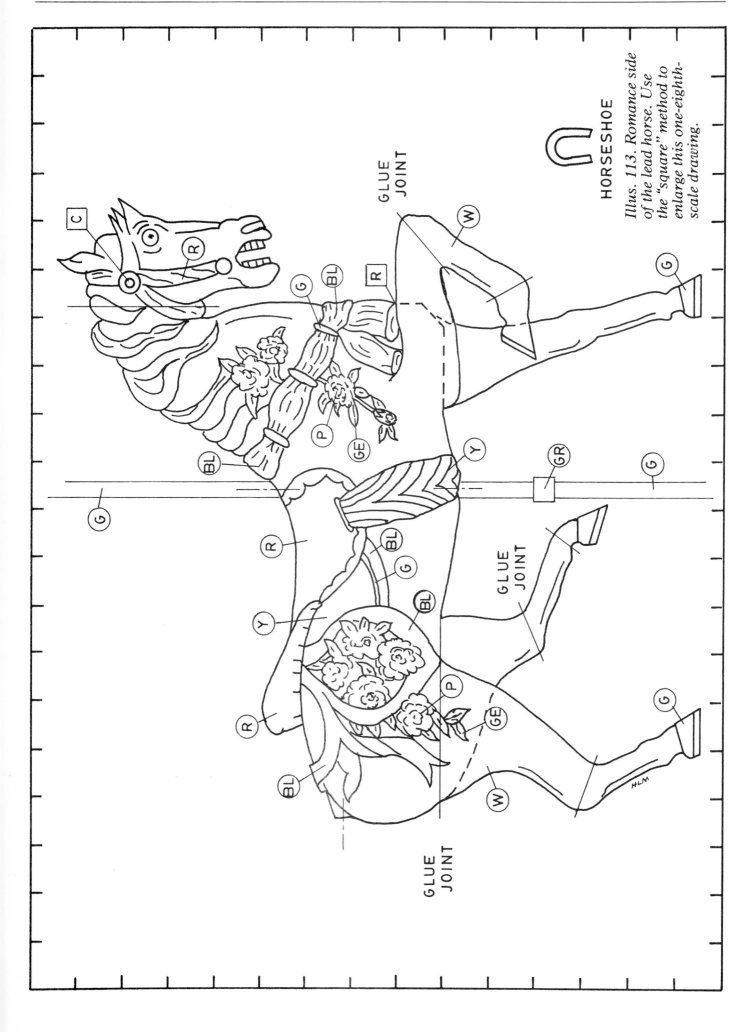

HORSESHOE

Illus. 113. Romance side of the lead horse. Use the "square" method to enlarge this one-eighth-scale drawing.

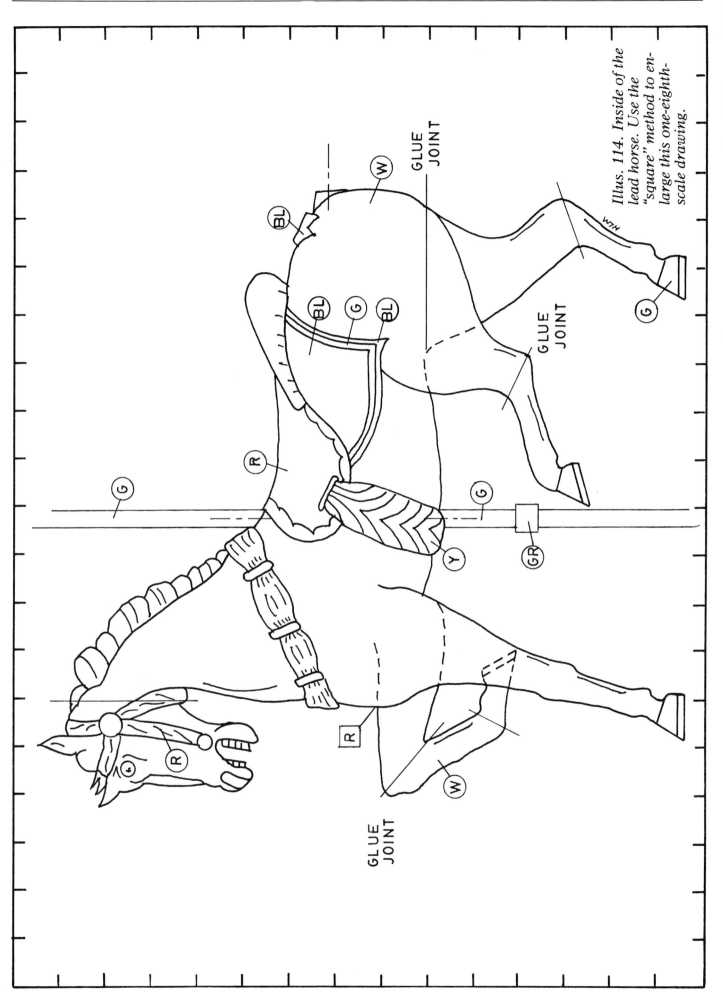

Illus. 114. Inside of the lead horse. Use the "square" method to enlarge this one-eighth-scale drawing.

The original carousel animals were not thought of as works of art, but as utilitarian objects. In many cases, the body and legs were quite boxy. You may want to consider this in your carving and depart from a true reproduction by giving a more natural or pleasing shape to your animal.

CARVING THE ROSES

Carve each rose separately and glue it to the body and neck of the horse. Do not carve the roses from a solid block because the grain structure will be too delicate to withstand the abuse a carousel rider may give it. Carve each petal separately and then assemble them. One way to make the roses is to follow the dimensions and shapes presented in Illus. 115.

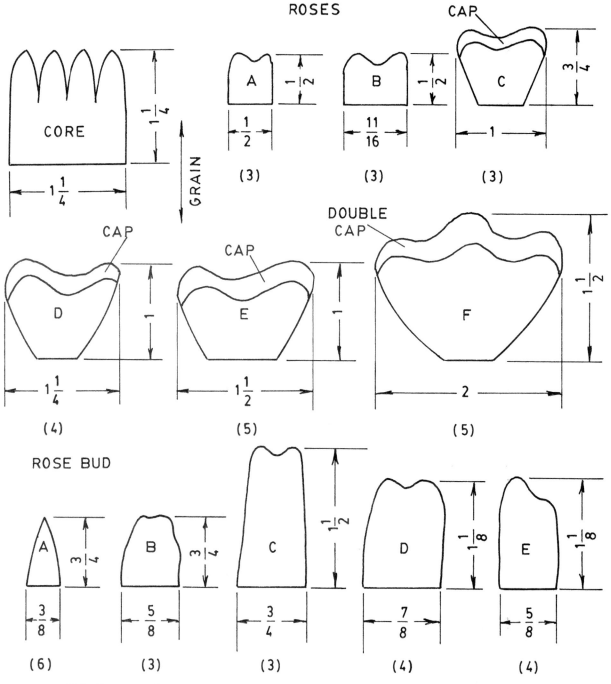

Illus. 115. Rose petal patterns.

Illus. 116. Close-up of roses on neck of full-size lead horse.

Illus. 117. Close-up of roses on rear of full-size lead horse.

Make each petal from one or more sections of 1/16" basswood. Basswood is not readily available in this thickness, so it will be necessary to produce your own. Cutting thin stock on a table saw can be dangerous, so be sure to follow all of the safety precautions of the tool manufacturer. Add an auxiliary wood fence to the rip fence. This will protect your blade if you accidentally get too close. Install a fine-tooth blade and set the distance between the fence and the blade at 1/16". Cut a piece of stock at least 1½" × 3" × 18" into enough 1/16" thick sheets to make the nine roses.

Make each rose the same way, although the outside diameters will vary because some of the roses are more open than others. Make eight roses and one rosebud. The roses on the top and bottom of the ribbon loop on the rear flank have the largest diameters, 3½". The rose on the front leg is 3¼" in diameter, and the roses on the front and rear of the ribbon loop and on the rear flank are 3". The two roses on the neck are 2¾", and the diameter of the rosebud is approximately 1".

To make each rose, cut out the parts as shown in Illus. 115. Pay particular attention to the direction of the grain. Soak the core in hot water and roll it tightly around a 3" length of ⅜" dowel. Place a rubber band around it to hold this shape until it is dry. When it is dry, wrap the core tightly around the dowel and glue it in place. Cut this dowel off when the rose is completed, but during construction use it as a handle.

Using a coping saw or jigsaw, cut out three small A petals. Soak them in hot water and bend them around a ⅜" dowel. When they are dry, equally space each petal around the core and glue it in place. Follow the same procedure to make three B petals, except in this case bend the petals around a ½" dowel.

Each C petal is made from two parts—the petal and a cap. Cut out three petals and three caps with a jigsaw. Soak them in hot water and bend them around a ½" dowel. When it is dry, glue the cap to the end of the petal as shown. Gently round the edge of the cap so that the petal is rolled back to resemble the curled edge of a rose. Space the petals equally around the B petals, fan the edges so that it looks as if the rose is opening, and glue the petals in place.

Petals D and E are made exactly like the C petals, except that D requires four petals and is bent around a 1" dowel, while E requires five petals and is bent around a 2" diameter form.

The F petals are the largest and form the final row of petals. Cut five petals and ten caps. Soak them in hot water and bend them around a 3⅜" diameter form. When they are dry, glue two caps to each petal. Round the front edges of the caps so that they are curled back. Space the F petals evenly around the E petals, fan out the edges to reach the required diameters, and glue the petals in place. You can achieve the finished diameter for each rose—from 2¾" to

3½"—by controlling the distance each row of petals fans out. Make certain that each petal is firmly glued in place. Cut off the dowel and flat-sand the back of each rose until there is an area of about 1" diameter. Glue the roses to the horse as shown in Illus. 111.

The rosebud (Illus. 115) is made in a manner very similar to that used for the roses. All parts are bent around a ½" dowel and the petals do not fan out. Start by cutting six A petals. Soak them in hot water and bend them around a ½" dowel. When they are dry, form a tight circle, with each petal overlapping. These six petals will form the core of the rosebud. Add the other petals as described above. When the bud is complete, shape the stem end and flatten a small area on one side near the stem. Glue the flat side against the horse with the bud point down.

MAKING A STAND

It is essential that the base be sturdy and heavy enough to hold the completed animal upright. The completed animal will weigh several hundred pounds and a person could be injured or the carving damaged if it is not supported properly. The main support is the pole. Several sizes and styles are available, and you may want to contact the suppliers listed on page 191 for detailed information.

Commercial stands for carousel animals can be purchased. However, you can add greater realism by making a base to resemble a segment of a full-size carousel platform as shown in Illus. 119. This base is 62" long and 24" wide. It is made of 2 × 4's covered by 3" tongue-and-groove flooring. It may be necessary to cut ⅜" deep saw kerfs every six inches or so into the front curved facing board to achieve uniform bending.

Illus. 118. A 1¾" hole saw is used to cut the hole in the body for the support pole.

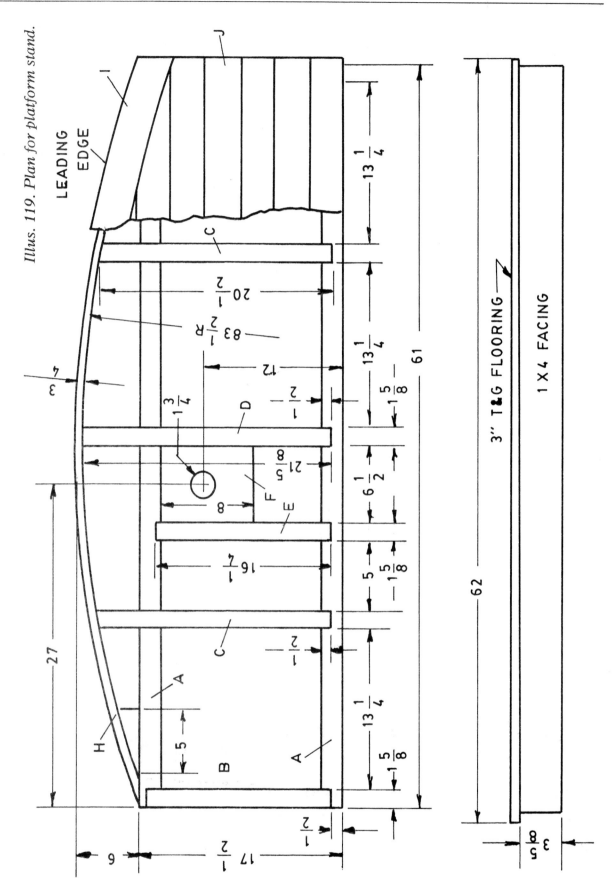

Illus. 119. Plan for platform stand.

Illus. 120. Support frame for full-size lead horse stand.

Drill a 1¾" hole into a piece of wood 3¼" × 6½" × 8". Glue a piece of ⅛" hardboard of the same size to the bottom. Glue this piece between the studs as shown. The hardboard will prevent the pole from scratching the floor.

When the 2 × 4 framework is completed, make the leading edge for the top from three pieces of ¾" stock. This edge overhangs the facing board by ½". Cover the framework with 3" tongue-and-groove flooring. If it is necessary to piece any of the floorboards together, the joints should occur in the center of the cross members. Cut the front section of the flooring to fit the curve of the leading edge. Table 63 is a list of materials needed to make the stand.

Table 63 Materials for the Lead Horse Stand

Part	Dimension	Number Required
A Longitudinal member	1⅝ × 3⅝ × 61"	2
B Cross member	1⅝ × 3⅝ × 16½"	2
C Cross member	1⅝ × 3⅝ × 20½"	2
D Cross member	1⅝ × 3⅝ × 21⅝"	1
E Cross member	1⅝ × 3⅝ × 16¼"	1
F Pole support	3¼ × 6½ × 8"	1
G Hardboard	⅛ × 6½ × 8"	1
H Facing	¾ × 3⅝ × 64"	1
I Leading edge	¾ × 3 × 22"	3
J Flooring	¾ × 3"	Approximately 9 square feet

The stand was finished with mahogany stain and satin finish varnish. The thickness of the leading edge was painted a bright red. It required approximately 25 hours to make and then to apply the finish to the stand.

FINISHING TOUCHES

For the lead horse pole, I used an 8′ length of 1¾" outside diameter pipe that can be purchased from a home supply dealer. It consists of one piece that goes through the horse and into the stand. The pipe is covered by a 2" outside diameter brass decorative sleeve. The sleeve is in two parts—the bottom section is 21½" long and the top

Illus. 121. Close-up of the support pole inserted into the body. Note the optional cross support rod and the corresponding carved recess in the underside of the body.

section measures 41¾". It is capped with a finial. Several styles of sleeves and finials are commercially available.

This horse has eleven ruby-red 15-mm jewels and one ruby-red 24-mm jewel in the front apron, and a sapphire-blue 15-mm jewel in the brow band. Glue these jewels in place after completing all of the painting.

The tail is a real horse's tail. It fits into the 1" hole in the rear flank. You can choose from several lengths, colors, and fullnesses of commercially available tails.

Illus. 122. A spade-shaped drill bit is used to make the 1" hole, into which a real horsehair tail will be inserted.

It is extremely important to seal the finished carving to prevent it from absorbing moisture. Household enamels work very well. Paint the body of the horse with four coats of a semi-gloss white enamel. Cut the first coat by ⅓ with thinner. Lightly sand between each coat. The colors suggested in Illus. 113 conform to the symbols listed on page 20. Since it is impossible to be certain of the original colors, you can select a color combination that is pleasing to you or one that complements the room decor where the carving will be displayed.

APPENDICES